THE MARILYNN KRAMAR STORY

The Marilynn Kramar Story
Joy Comes in the Morning

Marilynn Kramar
with
Robert C. Larson

Servant Publications
Ann Arbor, Michigan

Copyright © 1990 by Marilynn Kramar
All rights reserved.

Published by Servant Publications
P.O. Box 8617
Ann Arbor, Michigan 48107

Cover design by Michael Andaloro
Cover photo by Anacleto Rapping

90 91 92 93 94 10 9 8 7 6 5 4 3 2 1

Printed in the United States of America
ISBN 0-89283-655-5

Contents

Acknowledgments / 7
Preface / 9
Introduction / 11

1. The Birth of a Missionary Heart / 13
2. A Search for Direction / 35
3. Challenges in Colombia / 59
4. Pilgrimage of Truth / 83
5. The Price of Obedience / 107
6. Reconciliation / 125
7. A Promising Future / 133

Epilogue / 143

ACKNOWLEDGMENTS

I WANT TO THANK MY WHOLE FAMILY for being vulnerable in *The Marilynn Kramar Story*. It is my prayer that the story will be of great blessing and hope to you. Thanks especially:

To my father, who gave me the gift of self-assurance and inner strength;

To my mother, who put in me the "hope of heaven";

To Glenn, who gave me the happiness of being a wife and mother and who enabled me to open the door to the work of evangelization;

To Mark, who, as a beloved son, opened my eyes to my own weaknesses;

To Kimberly, who constantly makes me aware of the potential of being a mother;

To the family of CharisMissions, which has given me the courage not to give up, but to succeed;

To Cardinal Timothy Manning, who helped me trust in the "bird that flies"; and

To Esther Garzon, who through her love has given me back the confidence and assurance of being able to believe and live in friendship (Eccl 6:5-17).

Preface

"Tears may fall in the night, but joy comes in the morning."
Psalm 30:5

IN THIS BOOK, YOU WILL READ the story of a life filled with sadness, longings, and hope.

This is the story of a small flame that became, through the power and grace of God, an instrument he would use to light a tremendous fire in the world of evangelization. This is the story of Marilynn Kramar and of the dreams and miracles realized through a life totally given to God.

As you read this story, you will see how the realities of life knocked very hard at her door. Love, marriage, children, the calling of God to preach the Good News, disappointments, sadness, and broken dreams—all have been protagonists in this drama.

But for each dark cloud in her life, the Lord has sent her clear skies and rainbows. Healings, reconciliation, recovery, and peace have also been important players in this story. None other than Marilynn could tell us this story.

Her life has been a great blessing to many. It's our prayer that, through this book, it will be a blessing to thousands more.

—Staff of CharisMissions

INTRODUCTION

A Story to Tell

SHOES IN HAND, drenched in sweat, I walk toward the exit of the Los Angeles Sports Arena. It is the final night of the *Encuentro Latino*, the annual event of Catholic evangelization and renewal sponsored by CharisMissions.

As if I am watching a movie in my mind, I see thousands of faces, many of them wet with tears of repentance and aglow with expressions of joy. I recall that a large number of these brothers and sisters have traveled four days and nights by bus from the borders of Mexico and all twenty-three countries of the Spanish-speaking world. Participants have also come from all over the United States to share this three-day event of vibrant proclamations, profound worship, and consecrations to the Lord.

It's almost as if in my mind's eye, my own life flashes before me. What has brought me to this place, to this moment, in my life? How could one life be so full of sorrow and joy, and hope and heartache? From the moment of my conception in a family of love and faith to a time of severe testing, it has been a life of miracles and the pursuit of a dream.

How could one life be so intermingled with life's bittersweet reality and yet be so full of faith? From childlike discovery to tender love, from marriage and children to the missionary call and conversion, from hearing God's holy call to deep disappointment and shattered dreams of marriage and family life. Yet in the very moment of severe testing, I had discovered God's severe mercy in a time of recovery, peace, reconciliation, and healing—a healing that will only be complete when the Lord takes me home.

As I survey the sports arena one last time, I know that this is why I can address these thousands of brothers and sisters. God has hollowed out my heart and given me a missionary heart.

That is why I can take great joy in having shared the pulpit with CharisMissions evangelizers—young and old alike—who have been raised from the pits of drunkenness, divorce, and enslavement to be formed into the missionary heart of CharisMissions—ministries for evangelization that reach thousands through live rallies and radio and TV broadcasts.

Even as I take it all in one last time, it is almost as though the music still rings in my ears from the Christian artists and musicians who have been converted through CharisMissions and have sung new songs to the Lord in this very arena.

As I continue to make my way toward the exit, I fling my accordion over my shoulder, knowing it's time to get home to my pets—my cats Munkers and Bird Legs and my dogs Sasha and Popeye. I know they've endured a long weekend waiting at the door for my voice.

I break out of my reverie and to my surprise, notice there is a man waiting for me at the exit. It's Glenn, my former husband of twenty years. After having been through so much together, we greet with warmth. His embrace tells me once more, "You're a great lady. I'm so proud of you."

Yet as I walk to my car, I say to myself, "It's just the same old girl. What would I have done without your love, Jesus! Every moment has been worth it, and you're not finished with me yet, Lord. Together you and I have walked a long way. Let's just keep taking steps together. We truly have a life and a story to share."

ONE

The Birth of a Missionary Heart

THIS STORY BEGAN ON May 5, 1939, when I was born to Bill and Lorine Roberts after two five-year delays. And it didn't begin auspiciously. Five years after her marriage, my mother gave birth to a boy. But he died nine days later. To compound the grief, doctors told Lorine Roberts she could never have another child. But after much patience, prayer, and another five-year wait, God granted my parents a girl— me. Born in the seventh month, I, too, seemed destined to live an abbreviated life.

The date was the same month and day as the celebration of Mexican Independence day, *Cinco de Mayo*. This coincidence would lift my spirits many years hence.

Not only was my arrival two months premature, I was born with a deadly tumor on my neck. Some tendons were missing and this life-threatening tumor protruded on the outside of my neck. I spent three months in an incubator, and they tell me I cried almost constantly.

Most parents could easily have lost hope. But because of their strong faith, the Robertses were different and so was their approach to this trial.

Bill Roberts was raised on a farm in Idaho. Money was

tight, and he scarcely knew what a complete tablesetting was meant for. Mom, on the other hand, grew up in Southern California in a successful and affluent Swedish family. Her immigrant father and brothers ran a prosperous cabinet making shop. She would have enjoyed raising me with a silver spoon in my mouth.

But despite their divergent backgrounds, Bill and Lorine were joined in a common love for the Lord and his Word—so much so that my dad answered the call of Jesus to become a minister of a small congregation for the Assemblies of God church in Inglewood, California. His following grew into one of the largest Assemblies of God churches in southern California.

When Bill Roberts learned that his newborn daughter was not expected to live, he asked the congregation and a fledgling radio audience to join him in prayer. He and Lorine invited some of their close friends and fellow believers from the Assemblies of God church to come by for a prayer session. Following the example of Jesus and the apostles, some of them laid hands on me and prayed intently for my healing.

What happened next will never appear in any medical journals or science books. Barely three months old, I spent one of my first quiet, peaceful nights. In fact, I was so quiet that my parents began to wonder if their daughter had died in her sleep. But to the amazement and joy of all, I was healed. The tumor was gone. My neck appeared strong and normal. Even the X-rays and clinical examinations showed that I had a perfectly normal neck—so normal, in fact, I seem to have gone through life sticking it out and laying it on the line for others as if I believed nothing could harm the neck which God had healed!

Mom and Dad took me everywhere together. As a young child, I remember having lots of play time with the neighborhood kids. There were many opportunities for sports, and I especially enjoyed racing. God had given me quick legs, so I usually won. Maybe that's why kids often made me team captain when it came to choosing sides and playing games.

I still recall the delight of moving into our new home my parents built in west Los Angeles.

BEING THE PASTOR'S KID: THE GOOD TIMES

Being a pastor's kid is much like living in a rose garden. The privileges and opportunities can be as fragrantly sweet as rose petals at times, but the public scrutiny and high expectations can be as sharp as thorns.

I'll always treasure the sweet fragrance of the good times. I grew up as Dad's little sweetheart and the darling of the congregation. At an early age my neck and throat, so recently healed by God, supported a most beautiful singing voice. By the age of two, I was even singing on Dad's radio programs.

Music came easily for me, and Mother made sure I progressed. With much encouragement from her, I took up the piano, marimba, and accordion.

Coming from a rural background, my father introduced me to the joys of horseback riding. This encouraged a love for other outdoor activities such as cycling and even ice skating. Early life was a stream of delightful memories.

Every Saturday, as far back as I can remember, even though my dad was pastor of a church and very busy, was always "our day." He would plan Saturdays with me and dedicate the time to horseback riding, swimming, picnicking, and bike riding.

Every summer we traveled to the state of Idaho where my father's family lived on a farm in Twin Falls. There I learned how to run a tractor when I was only eight years old. While hunting for jackrabbits with my cousins and uncles, I became quite a sharpshooter. One time in the sagebrush I even ran into a rattlesnake. Instead of running away, I took the gun and shot it. Dad came running and cut off its head. When I brought back the rattles to Mom, she almost passed out to think little Marilynn had gotten so close to a deadly snake and attacked it.

Through experiences like this, Dad taught me not to be afraid. He cared for me with great attention and love as the only surviving child of his marriage. With him at my side I always felt that anything was possible.

If Dad imparted a passion for involvement, Mom imparted an awareness of precision, thanks to her Swedish background. Her humble, modest, exacting and God-fearing outlook on life was the perfect counterbalance to the easygoing approach I loved in my dad. Everything Mom did was organized and perfect. Every place setting was immaculate. Every meal was a balanced diet. She never forgot my vitamins. I remember always having to take Myladol (fish oil) every morning before going to school and at bedtime. She made sure I took piano lessons and from a very early age made me practice at least an hour a day. She even counted the minutes to make sure I didn't miss any.

Someone had to teach this youngster how to care for a proper parsonage, manage the finances, rear a family, and uphold the honor of the Lord's appointed servant—the pastor—to the congregation. But Mom was not entirely healthy. Recurring heart problems held her back. She was never quite able to keep up with my childish enthusiasm as well as Dad.

BEING THE PASTOR'S KID:
THE THORNS THAT PRICKED

The only thing more challenging than being a preacher's kid, is being the preacher's *only* kid. As I grew older, I began to prick myself on the ever-present thorns of public scrutiny with greater frequency.

There were little things at first. But soon they began to compound and inflict real discomfort. Why do they always have to look at me? Why do they always expect me to be a perfect angel? I was not afraid of the broadcast microphone, the church platform, or the high speed gallop on the horses I loved, but I began to panic at the relentless expectation of the congregation.

One time when I was attending vacation Bible school, I was tempted to steal one of my girlfriend's handiworks. It seemed much prettier than mine. So I replaced her name on the back with my own as if I had created this work of art. When I was discovered, everyone began to whisper and talk among themselves. Someone even told my mom. Then I got into real trouble.

What to do? Where to turn?

Age was also beginning to work its wonders. I found myself budding into an object of interest to the young men in the congregation, and I rebelled. I didn't run away or openly cast off the faith of my parents, I simply opened more distance between myself and the "spiritual" people in the congregation.

When you shun the light of grace it doesn't take long to find that you've stumbled into the shadows of sin. At the age of eleven, I began sneaking away from the eyes of the congregation every Sunday and meeting my boyfriends in the baptistry behind the pulpit where I remember my first kiss. Where others went to pray and immerse themselves in the Spirit, I went to immerse myself in youthful, amorous adventures.

It's not hard to imagine where such adventures would have led me had they not been cut short. Dad resigned from the pastorate when I was twelve. Soon Mom and I were looking for a new church and new friends. All of a sudden I was no longer the center of attention.

WHY HAVE YOU FORSAKEN ME?

Dad was always intense in ministry, but until this change he still had time for me. Gone were the days of waiting for

Dad out in front of the house where he would drive up from his church work, park the car, and reach out to catch the ball I was eagerly waiting to toss. Gone were the moments of simple pleasure.

What pulled Bill Roberts out of my life was a new venture called "The Far East Broadcasting Company." Working with associates such as John Broger and Bob Bowman, Dad was reaching believers in the Philippines, Russia, and China through a radio missionary outreach. After much prayer and soul-searching, he felt called to resign his position with the Inglewood church and pursue this missionary effort on a full-time basis. But the job was undefined. There was no sure income, no set schedule. He would have to leave Mom and me in California and travel a great deal overseas.

It was as if the Roberts family passed from a warm summer day to a cold winter night with no twilight or autumn in between. One day we had the security and prestige of being the minister's family. The next day we were laypeople in another man's congregation. For the first time in almost twenty-five years, my parents had to move and look for a new church home; and it seemed as though Mom and I were no longer in the limelight. We had to take second place not only in the eyes of our congregation, but also in my dad's heart because of all his new projects and programs for the cause of missionary radio.

Mom now made most of her decisions alone. Dad was gone much of the time and concentrated his energies on the new ministry. I was lonely for him and sometimes resentful.

At least these emotions took my mind off the burden of being the preacher's kid. Now I began to look forward to moving away from the Inglewood church and making a new life for myself as nothing more than "one of the crowd."

We took up a new church home at Bethel Temple, the mother church for the Assemblies of God in Los Angeles. But oh, how I missed my father.

To compensate for missing Dad, I think I paid a lot more

attention to my neighborhood friends. I remember playing in the streets with them until dark. We had a lot of happy times together, bike riding and planning weekend activities. All of my friends in the neighborhood were so close to me, they seemed to become almost like brothers and sisters.

At Christmas time, we would go from house to house and collect all of the Christmas trees after the twenty-fifth and pile them in my backyard. Then we would build a fort as big as the entire yard. We spent weeks imagining we were either campers or soldiers or someone else in the great outdoors.

Yet gone were the days of swimming, picnicking, and horseback riding with Dad. Every time I accompanied Mom to see Dad off at the airport for his extended trips of six weeks or more, I remember crying for weeks. One of the deepest sadnesses in my young life was knowing he was going to leave again and again. I felt my heart was breaking.

MOM'S RESOURCEFULNESS IN HARD TIMES

Mom was faced with equal challenges of her own. While Dad spent approximately nine months of the year on the road raising money for the ministry and spreading the gospel, precious little money came our way. Sometimes we sat in the house on the brink of starvation. We had to fend for our own income. Frequently God would bless the ministry with enough money so Dad could send us some. But when resources didn't materialize, we waited for checks and prayed.

I don't think I was that prayerful as a little girl, but I counted on Mom's prayers and that somehow the Lord would give us the wisdom to know what to do. I can remember neighbors who weren't even that close to us who would come and say, "God told us to bring this." One night we didn't know where we were going to eat, and one of my little friends asked his mother to invite us over for dinner with them.

Mom never seemed healthy enough to get a job. One time she tried a part-time job, but couldn't take the hours of standing on her feet. The only thing she really longed for was Dad and to be a pastor's wife again.

The plateaus of life are often framed by massive hills and valleys. Lorine Roberts had known ease and comfort before marrying Bill Roberts. Then starting together with very little, they built a comfortable life as the minister's family in Inglewood, California. Now Lorine was called upon once again to fabricate a living with virtually no resources.

Mom and I experienced no lack of resourcefulness. I remember her saving up pennies one time so she could buy me one pair of shoes to start school in September. She found a use for leftover plastic from her brother's cabinet-making business. She and I would make small molds and cut out flowers to adorn ordinary fly swatters. A little glue and needlework created a commodity I could take around selling door-to-door after school. Selling the fly swatters at one or two dollars apiece, we were able to earn enough money to buy a new outfit for both of us to wear to the General Council of the Assemblies of God and even pay for the trip.

A BEAU NAMED GLENN

One of the luminaries in the choir and music department at Bethel Temple was a boy named Earl Glenn Kramar. At the age of fifteen, he played the violin and the affections of Marilynn Roberts as well. He was always well dressed and seemed to want to be only with me. While he was polite about his interest in me, he would make gestures, like winking or turning his head my way, to indicate he liked me.

I was no longer the "preacher's kid" in the congregation.

Neither was I endowed with any burning desire to serve the Lord. Glenn arrived as an interesting diversion. We formed a singing group, which Glenn enjoyed. He seemed excited about everything I did—how I dressed, how I looked. He made it a point to compliment me and tell me how pretty I was.

His family lived on a citrus ranch in La Puente, California, and he had a younger sister named Evelyn. An older brother named John was so near to Glenn's age that people often asked, "Why can't you be as good and as smart as your brother?" Glenn often mentioned how tough it was being constantly compared to his brother. Glenn was always trying to prove he was as good as the other members of his family.

All in all, Glenn's was a fairly normal family of five. His mother, Edith, and father, John Willard, came from a Quaker background and work ethic. Both had become devoted lay ministers in the Assemblies of God. Glenn never seemed that close to his parents. In fact, he appeared somewhat ashamed that they were poorer than many families he knew. He seemed self-conscious because his father always dressed in farmer's clothes and never seemed to have friends around him who, in the eyes of the world, looked important. Glenn even seemed embarrassed about their ranch in La Puente.

I, for one, held Glenn's parents in the highest esteem. In fact, his mother, Edith, helped arrange an extremely important youth conference that introduced me to the most important man in my life—and his name wasn't Glenn.

ENCOUNTERING THE LAMB AT BIG BEAR

The youth conference took place in Big Bear, California. Glenn, of course, was there. And because of his encouragement, so was I. But the most important encounter for me that weekend was not with Glenn.

I still didn't want to mingle with those other kids who were interested in prayers and witnessing and other spiritual things. In fact, while they gathered down at the lodge for the nightly meetings, I kept to myself in the dorm, hoping they wouldn't come and drag me down there to pray with them.

But Evelyn, Glenn's younger sister, didn't accept my behavior. One evening she came looking for me and found me relaxing in flannel pajamas.

"Marilynn, why don't you come down and pray with us?" she asked.

Unwilling to give an inch on my personal commitment to noncommitment, but equally unwilling to say no to a friend and miss out on the action, I agreed to go.

"Okay, I'll go down there. But just for you," I said.

Because I had planned to hide in the back of the room, I didn't even bother to change clothes or put on a bathrobe. However, something must have worked its way to the back of the room because, all of a sudden, I felt myself beginning to talk to the Lord openly in prayer. This was something I hadn't done in a long time. I began to say, "Okay, Lord, whatever you want of me!" I was overcome by the Spirit for a full three hours. The only way to describe it is to say that I felt as if the Lord Jesus had wrapped me in his arms and had pressed me close and said, "I love you, I love you, and I need you." I found myself answering back, "I love you, too."

Though I grew up in a Christian family, I had never been able to make a personal, public profession. I remember the many times I had wanted to make a public step of faith and go to the altar. But I always felt that someone was watching and would be surprised that a preacher's kid didn't already know Jesus. I would end up staying back and watching the others, and then go back to my room at home and offer my own little prayers in private. Perhaps it was the loss of Dad's closeness. Or maybe it was the fear of someone watching me.

I don't really know what stopped me for so many years from taking this step of faith. Perhaps it was the financial pressure or other people's demanding expectations. Perhaps it was guilt. But now all of that seemed to vanish.

The next thing I knew, three hours had passed. All the others had gone to bed, leaving me alone with the Lamb of God. He had confronted the beast of confusion and won. What a difference! Where before I had enjoyed the outdoors because of my free spirit as a sports enthusiast and my love of spending time with my friends, now I walked out by myself under the dramatic night sky in the mountains. I gazed off in the distance to a group of lights in the plains below. It seemed that I was seeing for the first time the candles of God above and the lights of his creation below. I felt a tremendous enthusiasm ignite within me that has not diminished to this day.

I remember thinking, "I have to tell everyone that Jesus loves them just as he loves me."

MY FIRST STEPS IN THE LORD

But how does a fifteen-year-old girl find an outlet for such conviction? Where does she go to witness for Jesus? How and when?

I went back and began to share my excitement with a lot of the kids at church. But they weren't deeply involved in any particular mission. They were simply "good kids." With this newfound zeal I realized there was something within me that was special. I deeply wanted to express what had happened.

Fortunately, I had a friend, Gladys Pearson, who was a wonderful preacher of the Word, a woman missionary. I always admired her zeal. She had been a friend of my family for years and had shared the pulpit with my father and many other ministers of churches in the Assemblies of God. She had traveled for years as a missionary. Whenever she came to our church, she always stirred my desire to consecrate my life to Christ and to become an evangelist or a missionary myself.

Naturally, Gladys picked up on what was happening to me and invited me to walk with her on the streets of Los Angeles. So I did.

One night we found ourselves on Fifth and Main. Gladys said to me, "Marilynn, why don't you tell these people what the Lord has done for you? You can do it."

Before me was a small crowd of drunks and prostitutes. They reminded me of the times my father had taken me down to the streets of Los Angeles to show me what the world was really like. He wanted me to understand sin and its consequences. Now I was faced with the opportunity to do something about the situation.

"Okay, I'll do it," I finally said.

Saying that to Gladys was the easy part. Coming up with something to say to this calloused audience was another matter. There I stood. I don't remember how I started out. Maybe I sang a little song or something of that sort because that has always been characteristic of me. But whatever I did, people started coming and listening. I remember feeling deeply impressed about their needs.

I went back to our church and began to recruit other kids to go out on the streets with us. We began to look for ways to visit the destitutes in Los Angeles missions. Then I received invitations to sing and preach in the downtown missions. We began making it a regular occasion to go down and serve these people on Monday nights.

Glenn was part of the group and shared my love for these people in need. In fact, he helped me pack up a cake and share my own birthday with these downtrodden people who often wondered if they had seen their last birthday.

One of them made a lasting impression: an elderly man who had been in prison for about thirty years and had just been released. He was extremely sad and lonely. He explained to me how he had lost his family, all of his possessions, and his home as well. When I spoke or sang, he would sit there and cry. He mentioned that I sometimes reminded him of the family he had lost. Experiences like that strengthened my resolve to give my heart and my life to help the needy people of our world.

A CALL TO COMMITMENT AND MARRIAGE

During these shared experiences I found myself drawing closer and closer to Glenn Kramar. In addition to the church activities, Glenn enjoyed sharing time with my family as well. On those rare occasions when my father was home from the Far East, Glenn would make himself right at home. The relaxed atmosphere of my family was a welcome contrast to the more structured lifestyle of the Kramars. Glenn could sit and talk for hours, even when I wasn't there. He felt as if he belonged.

We seemed destined for an early marriage. He was seventeen, I was only sixteen, and both of us had a great deal of maturing to do. I should have known it wasn't time to make a serious commitment toward marriage, seeing with my own eyes some of the special limitations and problems that seemed to be expressed in Glenn's life.

On one occasion, after friends from church teased him about some insignificant matter, he disappeared for hours and didn't tell me where he was going or what he was doing. On another occasion, he became jealous of me and the relationship I had with my neighborhood friends. In his rage, he would knock his head against the car and scare me until I begged him to stop hurting himself.

Expressions such as these should have warned me that we weren't ready to make a serious commitment toward marriage, but I really felt I loved him. I wanted a husband and male figure in my life in order to feel complete. Glenn was there, and in spite of these problems, he was interested in me and the work of the Lord. Before I knew what was happening, we were engaged.

Events happened so fast. Our love for one another was the most important thing in our lives—except that he was required to fulfill his military obligation. So we became engaged and parted for two years, while Glenn served in the Navy.

WAITING WASN'T EASY

I was a teenager of sixteen and Glenn was a long way off. I had a lot of good times during his absence, but one relationship in particular was not what it should have been.

I wanted to work after school and save some money. So I found a job at the J.C. Penney Company. They not only gave me the job but really liked my work. I was thrilled to have money of my own.

Every afternoon I had to walk from school to work in front of a used-car lot. The assistant manager was quite a bit older than I, but somehow he began to attract my attention and interest. Maybe I saw him as a father figure. Maybe he represented the strong masculine partner I sought. Maybe I was lonely.

Soon we began passing more than the time of day. I thought I had learned a great deal about romance from my boyfriends in Inglewood church. But this veteran knew how to sell more than used cars!

I would meet him after work and we would sit in the back of the used car lot. I was awakened for the first time to sexual desires I never realized could be felt. His words and caresses made me feel overwhelmed with desire for him. I longed for the next chance to be with him.

While we never consummated these desires, in my mind I found myself thinking about him and longing for him. No one had ever made me feel as beautiful as he did. Sometimes he came into J.C. Penney's, and my heart would leap.

Every day I would write to Glenn somewhere in the Pacific. And every day I would look forward to my next meeting with this newfound friend. This internal contradiction of almost two years impeded my contact with the Lord for a while. It should have warned me that my union with Glenn was not as firm as it could have been.

However, all was not shadows. During this two-year engagement, we shared the sunshine of daily letters. We never missed a day of writing to each other. Looking toward the future, we joyously shared the excitement of planning a life together. All of this buoyed the life of a bride-to-be.

MRS. GLENN KRAMAR

Soon Glenn returned from the Navy and our wedding day approached.

Three days before our marriage, one event took place that should have given me cause for serious concern. Glenn flew into one of his jealous rages and proceeded to vent his wrath by knocking his head against the wall at my home. He seemed to feel unworthy of being my husband and insecure about his ability to be a good provider.

"I don't want to marry him! I want to call it off!" I cried to my mother.

But Mom brought us both into the house, sat us down, and had us talk out the whole situation. Promises were made, and tempers cooled. The marriage went on.

Looking back from this point of reference, it might be easy to say we should never have married. But that could easily miss the mark of God's hand in our lives. At Glenn's side, I followed the will of the Lord through hundreds of experiences that helped thousands of people.

28 / *The Marilynn Kramar Story*

We cannot choose our parents or our immediate family. So it is with the hand of the Lord. Many times we are caught up in situations that the Lord somehow uses and cannot choose our fellow bond slaves.

Miss Marilynn Roberts, age eighteen, became Mrs. Glenn Kramar on August 3, 1957. My father, Pastor William Roberts, conducted the ceremony.

CALLED BY THE LORD

Looking at my parents' lives, Glenn and I had decided that the rigorous life of ministry was not for us. Glenn had always wanted to obtain a degree in business administration and work in the world of commerce. He planned on getting his degree from the University of California at Los Angeles. I got a job at the Los Angeles County Museum as an executive secretary for the curator of history.

My days were full of excitement, and I loved the work. I also learned a lot about organizing exhibitions. In fact, I even worked for the museum on the side modeling antique clothes for museum exhibits. All of this filled my life with a special joy—except for the day I received my first paycheck.

With that first paycheck I went out and bought myself a beautiful new dress. As soon as I got home, I put it on for Glenn. His response was not what I expected.

He flew into a rage and told me, "How could you spend twenty-six dollars for a dress? Don't you know we need that money to help put me through college?" My joy at having been able to buy something pretty was deflated by my husband's fury.

Even so, our life went on. Glenn was now studying intently at UCLA, and I was enjoying my work at the museum, that is, until one fateful night at Bethel Temple.

It was almost midnight on a Saturday in December. What was it the visiting evangelist had said? "The Good News has not been heard by all." Glenn was sure he had heard that statement many times from that same pulpit. Why then this discomfort, this restlessness in his heart?

Glenn had come to the front of the church alone after the service, leaving me on the other side praying. There the questions had begun—questions that cast a probing white light on our new life together and how we fit into God's plan. What were we doing? Where were we going?

After what seemed like hours in prayer, Glenn heard a voice from within him, one he had come to recognize.

"Here is where I want you." Then he was beckoned with an irresistible call to approach the pulpit in the center of the church. As he obeyed and moved toward the steps leading to the pulpit in the now silent, nearly darkened church, Glenn was confident he was hearing a call to proclaim the gospel of Christ.

Stunned and awed, he replied, "Well, Lord, if that's what you want, I'll do it."

But now he wondered. Glenn felt comfortable with things of commerce and business administration. He knew he was capable in that field. And, equally as sure, he knew he was incapable of the things required of a minister. He was painfully shy with strangers and awkward in public situations. When called upon to speak before any but the closest friends, his heart pounded and his throat closed down so that he could hardly breathe. Yet, as he stood behind the pulpit of Bethel Temple, he felt confident that the call to preach was not to be fulfilled behind that one familiar pulpit alone, but in many other pulpits as well.

Then he became concerned about how to tell me. We had been married only four months and were only now beginning to live out the plans we had made for several years. In all the countless hours together, we had never considered that he might preach.

And yet Glenn was confident this was the will of the Lord. Not comprehending how it could be, he threw himself into the arms of Jesus and said, "Yes."

Across the church, I prayed alone. We always prayed separately in church so that each would feel free to express our own feelings. Glenn prayed to himself, while I was often more expressive.

In the silence, I began to sense a moving of the Spirit within me. For a moment I was afraid because I suspected God was asking for a more complete dedication. I knew from my parents how busy a life could be when given to God and how obedient to the Spirit one must be. Glenn and I were in agreement that we would never follow that way of life.

And yet God was speaking directly to me. He seemed to be saying, "You truly are my children, and I have a plan for your lives far beyond what you have considered or even imagined. Give yourselves back into my hands, and I will show you what to do."

I had the feeling I was not being asked to be only a minister's wife. There was a "global" feeling about this call—an expansiveness to it that extended beyond Los Angeles.

Would I be willing to change my plans and allow the Lord to show me a different direction, a path Glenn and I both had said we would not follow?

The still, small voice was so compelling that there was nothing to be said but, "Yes, Lord." And with this assent, peace and joy flooded into my soul.

"But, Lord," I continued, "you'll have to speak to Glenn yourself because he has his heart set on going into business, and it would be impossible for me to convince him of another type of life."

On the way home to the rows of apartments where we lived, I dared to speak about this newly formed conviction. "Honey, let's not go in for a while. I have something to tell you." I took a deep breath and prayed silently for the words. "Tonight in prayer I felt the Lord was telling me to consider a different type of life than what we've been thinking of, and I feel he is calling us to a full-time ministry."

Glenn turned to me with a slight grin and said, "Honey, don't worry about it, because he spoke to me, too."

We hugged and laughed and cried and talked, then laughed and cried again. We asked ourselves in stunned wonder, what could he want from us and what could we possibly do? We were mere kids of nineteen and twenty and couldn't imagine ourselves ministering the Word of God.

"Oh, God, forgive us for saying we could never be ministers," I remember praying. I'm confident he answered that prayer. But I sometimes wish we had probed more diligently for *how* the Lord intended for us to serve.

FROM UCLA TO PASADENA

Glenn immediately packed up his secular books and purchased the theological texts he would need for seminary classes at the Nazarene college in Pasadena. He also took jobs dressing window mannequins at J.C. Penney's, selling shoes, and other assorted jobs to support his long preparation for the ministry.

Glenn and I continued weekly services for the disadvantaged in Los Angeles. We also decided to hold meetings in the street as well as the mission building. Although Glenn seemed shy in so many ways, he became more and more open to sharing the Good News in a public way. With each opportunity to minister, he became more confident in himself and in his capacity to share with others.

Once again Monday night became mission night. Glenn and I helped conduct services for homeless men during their evening meal. Sometimes other ministers came; often we were there alone. This was a captive audience, but love and need on both sides soon made it an experience we all looked forward to sharing.

I would play the piano and Glenn would lead the songs.

Once again I held a birthday party with this special congregation. There were nineteen candles. I was still a teen, but growing up fast in the knowledge of the Lord.

Glenn was still active in the youth group at Bethel Temple in Los Angeles and decided to share the mission experience with them. He wanted to hold meetings in the street instead of the mission building.

The first Monday night, sixteen kids from the church came down with their tambourines and other assorted musical instruments and began singing under the blinking sign announcing "Beds for 50 Cents." A small crowd gathered, and after a while I stopped the music and Glenn stepped out to share spontaneously.

"Since I've known Jesus, everything in my life is different, and I know he can change every life here."

Glenn's love for people seemed obvious, and those on the street seemed to listen intently to this young man. His neatly trimmed hair, polished shoes, and sports jacket would have set him worlds apart from the "Jesus Freaks" that, in a few years, would have such an impact on the drug-ridden society of the 1960s. But his message was the same: the transforming power of Jesus. We teens from Bethel were not following any pattern we had been taught; we were simply following the lead of our own hearts a few years before such activity was to become a national phenomenon.

Grace was falling all around the streets of Los Angeles' skid row section. Many people came to Bethel Temple and then all the way home to Christ through those street meetings and the workings of a husband-and-wife team who weren't even ordained ministers.

Perhaps the reason so many came to listen and stayed to believe was that there was a different tone to our message than what they usually heard. Glenn and I vividly remembered the harangues of hellfire and brimstone from other preachers. Here we could study the faces of the people who stood to listen and know that behind the hardened, scornful eyes were people longing for acceptance, security, and relief from the all-pervasive fear that already haunted them. Accusations, shame, and threats would only cause the shell to close more tightly in an attempt to blot out the fear and remorse. Only hope, assurance, and love could dissolve such armor.

A MOVE TO MISSOURI

I expected an orderly life around my husband's systematic preparation for the ministry at the Nazarene college in Pasadena. This tidy routine lasted precisely one year.

After counsel with the pastor of our church, we came to the conclusion that our intentions were to join the pastoral ranks of the Assemblies of God. We felt Glenn should finish seminary in the headquarters' school of the church in Springfield, Missouri. The Assemblies of God seminary would furnish a more complete education than possible at a college of another denomination in Southern California.

Within a matter of weeks, we had sold our furniture and practically all of the household possessions we had received as wedding gifts and were pulling a U-Haul trailer to Springfield, Missouri.

Upon arrival at the college, we found that the apartments for married couples were former Army barracks, a far cry from the tidy apartment I had enjoyed in California. I remember doing all I could to soften the spartan, broken-down, military atmosphere and dumpy place, so Glenn could concentrate on his higher lessons of the Lord. But somehow, his attention became diverted to another interest.

TWO

A Search for Direction

MY BEST FRIEND AT SEMINARY in Springfield, Missouri was a secretary who lived three or four doors from our apartment in a trailer. We worked together as secretaries for the headquarters of the Assemblies of God in Springfield. We spent a great deal of time together and it seemed we had a lot in common, through sports, the local health club, and as family friends. Her husband was Glenn's friend and classmate at the seminary. Naturally, Glenn was well acquainted with her also—too well acquainted.

One night I was expecting Glenn to come home late in the evening. When he didn't arrive on time I went to bed without him. Out of the darkness came a strong awareness—strong enough and clear enough to wake me suddenly. "Oh, no. Glenn is having an affair with my best friend!"

It didn't seem real or possible. But when I woke up and began thinking about the situation, I imagined how it might be true. I had noticed their many loving glances and the times Glenn made excuses to drop by their trailer home for some insignificant reason.

So I asked him.

"Yes," he said and admitted that he was in a full-blown affair with her. This seemed to shatter all of my dreams and confidence.

In one swift pass, the razor of infidelity severed a friendship for good and wounded a marriage. From out of that open wound flowed a hemorrhage of doubt and confusion. Where did I fail to meet his emotional and physical needs? Are there other women I don't even know about? What will become of our marriage? Our soon coming baby? How can I remain faithful to a man who isn't faithful to me? What about our commitments to the Lord? Who knows about this affair? What's going to happen to us?

Beverly cried on the phone when I asked her if it was true. She begged me to forgive her and told me it was more important to have me as a friend than to ever see Glenn again. But it was too late. Although I would someday forgive her, we would never remain close friends.

The questions poured in like flood waters, but the answers advanced like a glacier. Over the hours, days, and weeks, the warm glow of God's love and forgiveness started to thaw the ice. After a while, I began to realize from my own involvement with the used-car salesman during our engagement that perfect love and loyalty are essentially gifts from God. They don't happen automatically. To paraphrase the Scriptures, God tells us: "If you love someone, you will be loyal to him no matter what the cost. You will always believe in him, always expect the best of him, and always stand your ground in defending him" (1 Cor 3:17 LB).

These attributes are impossible with human love. But when two people sincerely want the love of God shed abroad in their hearts, then they can endure, and they can forgive.

Fortunately, Glenn was truly contrite. He wanted to change. He wanted to resume his walk with the Lord toward the goal we shared.

"Darling, can you ever forgive me?"

"No, Glenn I can't—not alone," I thought to myself. "But I can do all things through Christ who strengthens me. Help thou my unbelief, and the forgiveness will come."

Sin can be so quick and easy. But, oh, how the consequences of it can linger and complicate our lives.

PREPARATION FOR OUR SERVICE TO THE LORD

"Mother," I once wrote back home to Los Angeles. "What in the world am I going to do about Glenn? He just doesn't seem to be able to preach with security. He'll never be like Dad. He worries so much about his messages, even sweats it out, and becomes so uncomfortable before he has to give his sermons."

Mother always seemed to encourage me. She told me of her own experiences with Dad when he was also was having a struggle with preaching. She told me, "Don't worry, dear. When your dad started out, there were twelve people in his congregation. After his first sermon, six of them walked out and never came back. If the Lord could do it for your father, he can do it for Glenn, too."

The months expanded into two years. The hard work and study continued. Whatever God intended for us, he seemed to be in no hurry to reveal. As Glenn graduated from seminary, he still had a hard time expressing himself to strangers. After our previous "missionary" work on the streets, he was effective, but still not completely comfortable with others.

Soon there would be a new arrival in the Kramar family who would give us an opportunity to practice the Word twenty-four hours a day. On September 11, 1961, I gave birth to William Marcus Kramar—one of the happiest days of my life.

Glenn and I remained home in Los Angeles for one semester and lived with my parents, while Glenn took a job at the Post Office. After six months we saved enough money to return to Springfield for the final semester of seminary.

When we arrived, Glenn continued to study and also took a part-time job in a bakery in Springfield. I stayed home with Mark and cherished the hours with him. I remember the many walks with him in the stroller and the precious hours I spent watching him grow.

Mark was an aggressive little child. He never liked to

sleep much and kept me up most of the night listening to him play in his crib. Mark's first year was tough on me because I found myself enveloped in his life and his needs. I enjoyed the challenge of this energetic little baby, but at times I felt my own inadequacy in knowing how to take care of him. It was challenging because I was an only child and had never had brothers and sisters.

While my circumstances as a stay-at-home mom did not allow me the opportunity to gain formal skills in the ministry, I cherished every occasion to advance informally. I would study on my own and, as best I could, learned techniques in the area of preaching from Glenn's books on homiletics.

As graduation approached, it seemed that Glenn Kramar's seminary diploma was going to be enable us to do the Lord's work and serve anywhere we chose. Or was it?

OUR RETURN TO CALIFORNIA AND OUR LAUNCH INTO MINISTRY

Our first calling was an invitation from Pastor Roberts (Grandpa) in northern California. There in the city of Belmont was a Latin American branch of the Far East Broadcasting Network and the Voice of Friendship for Latin America.

Our duties included both promotional work for the radio ministry as well as administration in the actual daily work of radio station KGEI. Both Glenn and I gained experience in speaking before diverse groups of supporters and raising money for overseas outreach. We found ourselves behind many microphones in churches sharing the work of the Far East Broadcasting Company. Glenn seemed to take to this work, although it was difficult to have to speak in new situations before new audiences. But this distant missionary work didn't stir the blood of a couple fresh out of seminary who found themselves wanting more of a direct assignment with the flock.

The small city of Concord was a storybook town of thirty-seven thousand near Oakland and San Francisco in northern California. There a position opened up for an associate pastor of the Assemblies of God church. We jumped at this opportunity to put our training to work. Surely this was where God was calling us.

Glenn became youth pastor (the group consisted of twelve members), and I was put in charge of the music department. It was an instant love affair between congregation and the young assistant pastor and his wife. However, we failed to notice how the mounting pressures of illness and advanced study were taking their toll on the senior pastor. This insensitivity, at least in part, led to significant problems later with the senior pastor and his wife.

The youth group began to grow from the twelve members. Soon there were from seventy-five to one hundred active teenagers coming every week to work in various activities and outreaches. They grew rapidly in number, not only because of our tender loving care, but also due to the many youth outreaches and weekend missions we sponsored on the streets. I remember many outings with these joyous young people: snow trips, picnics, and various social events. All of this was a vibrant part of our youth program for this Assemblies of God church, and we were enjoying every minute of it.

Then Kimberly Regina Kramar joined our household on November 5, 1964. We had wanted a little girl, and she was our dream come true. Kimberly was easy to take care of. Her brother Mark, now three years old, loved her dearly.

I was especially blessed with a family who helped me with the children. I began again two weeks after the birth of Kimberly to help Glenn with the ministry of the church. It was only possible because of the help I had at home from this family and other church members.

These were some of our happiest days as a family. We bought our first home and lived somewhat as a normal family. I remember the many hours we traveled on our day off to San Francisco and other locales with the kids. There were lots of picnics and outings, not just with Kimberly and Mark, but with other young couples from the church. During this time, we learned how to go camping from some of the younger families in the church. They took us on trips and taught us how to put up a tent and how to rough it in the great outdoors.

Remembering the Los Angeles skid row experiences, Glenn and I decided to lead the young people into active ministry. I taught them many songs and helped Glenn train them in how to give testimony and talk about their faith. The kids themselves began to give seminars and retreats to little children (called "kids' crusades") and to teach vacation Bible school. These budding evangelists also ventured out into the streets on Friday nights not for cruising and drinking with most of the other kids their age in Concord, but for singing and witnessing.

Finally, there was a month-long missionary journey into Mexico. Taking fifteen kids in two trailers, we went from town to town, visiting Assemblies of God churches. More than half of those teenagers today are in active ministry, at least in part, because of this outreach.

These were years of deep satisfaction. We experienced love and acceptance. But after three years, we began to be discontented with our situation. Part of it was simply a desire to have a congregation of our own.

Another part was that the senior pastor at Concord seemed preoccupied and distant. Further, although his wife was always supportive, she was often reserved. Perhaps it was the Lord's way of telling us it was time to make a move.

On a particularly beautiful morning, I remember bundling Kimberly into her traveling clothes and joining Glenn and

Mark for a drive through a new area that was opening up nearby in Danville, California.

Where only months before had stood giant, old trees and an occasional farmhouse, there were now bulldozers and cement mixers busily clearing a path for what was then considered the move of progress.

"Honey, I don't think there's a church within miles of here," Glenn said. "What do you think?"

"I think the first one will be ours."

GOD REVEALS HIS WILL UNEXPECTEDLY

Gladys Pearson was what we might call in the Catholic church a spiritual director. She had always been a part of our ministerial life, especially because of her evangelistic experiences from our youth. She happened to be ministering at a church in Northern California near Concord so we decided to go see her and share our dreams.

I was so excited about the prospects at Danville, I had to share the news with someone. Gladys was always interested. In fact, on several occasions she had challenged me to improve my life of service in the ministry.

"Why aren't you developing your preaching skills?" she would ask.

"I don't think I'm ready to do that," I would tell her, somehow suspecting that too much drive on my part might distract Glenn from his responsibilities and growth.

But here was some news Gladys was sure to appreciate. We met her one evening while she was holding a meeting in nearby Stockton.

She hugged us with great affection. Then as we sat on the sofa, we brought her up to date on what God had done for us and where we felt we were going. We poured out our hearts and dreams of a new church in Danville. Gladys sat and listened without changing her expression.

When the last plan had been shared, the last enthusiastic dream recounted, Gladys pulled herself upright and fixed us with a long, steady look. "Are you finished?" she asked.

"Yes," Glenn answered.

"Whatever are you thinking of?" she exploded. "Who are you thinking of? Is that the reason you became ministers, so that you could have the most successful church in Concord or Danville? Or did you become ministers to serve God in the most effective way?"

I was unable to speak. Glenn was white with anger.

Finally, I asked, "Gladys, why are you saying these things to us?"

"Because I think you are being very selfish," Gladys answered. "Where is your vision? For the very same amount of energy you might put forth in the United States, you could give yourselves to Latin America or India and have a hundredfold in comparison to what you would have here, even with a very successful church. I've ministered around the world, and I know where the greatest needs are."

"God hasn't called us to go around the world," Glenn said. He was furious with her and wounded by the unexpectedness of her reaction. "We're serving God. We can't go anywhere unless he puts the call into our hearts."

Glenn took Mark's hand, now a child of four, looked at our one-year-old, Kim, and headed for the door. "There are needs everywhere, including Danville. We're not missionaries. That's not our calling."

The drive from Stockton to Concord was unusually quiet. I sat beside Glenn holding Kim asleep in my arms. Neither of us spoke. As Glenn negotiated the curves of the winding road down into the valley, I suddenly understood.

So I turned to Glenn and quietly said, "She's right, you know. It's really true."

The experiences with the youth groups in Mexico came rushing back into my memory. I remembered the people we had ministered to, the children abandoned because their mothers and fathers had not enough love to share with them. The hunger—physical and spiritual—we had seen in the eyes of the hundreds of destitute people who had come to hear a word of hope. I remembered the stories my father had told of his experiences in the Philippines. The needs of people from all around the world came rushing in on me.

"Dear God," I remember praying silently. "Did you bring us together with Gladys Pearson today to show us something that we hadn't thought of before?" As I said the words, I knew it was so. Gladys had spoken the Lord's word to us.

"She's right," I repeated to Glenn.

"I think she is," he said with a cautious grin. "I hate to admit it, but I think she's right."

We both remembered our call at Bethel Temple where Glenn received the impression he was going to speak in many pulpits. Now I began to realize there was a "global" dimension to our calling. I looked down at Kim and Mark, now asleep, and wondered what life would hold for them and for us. They were so happy in their new home in Concord and had so many little friends. I felt the pangs of the unknown loom before me as I wondered what this decision would cost us as well as them.

PREPARING FOR THE MISSIONS

By the time the decision was made, it already seemed like the most natural thing to do. The Kramar and Roberts families had been missionary-oriented. John Willard had shown Glenn the work of a missionary in his own small part of the world. Glenn's parents had always been involved in lay ministries, working especially with minority groups, such as Hispanics and Russians in Southern California.

Pastor Roberts' wife had had to leave her comfortable pastorate in Los Angeles to bring the gospel to the Far East, and the heritage of Bethel Temple was clearly missionary to both of our families.

As we shared our decision with Gladys, she began to speak to us about Latin America. I remembered what she told us: "For the same energies that you would put out to pastor a church in California, if you went to Latin America or to India, you could multiply these energies a hundredfold." Now we were searching for that answer.

We zealously threw ourselves into the search for a destination with zeal. "Lord, somewhere in this world is a special job you've made just for us. There are people whom you love and who are waiting for that love to be shown through us. Give us your grace and show us the way," we asked God. Day after day, waiting on the Holy Spirit to guide, this prayer ascended to God. And day after day our interest grew in Latin America.

We read much about the cultures of each Latin American country. Colombia stood out in our minds for several reasons. First, it was one of the most conservative Catholic countries in Latin America—a field ripe for harvest from our Pentecostal perspective. It was a growing country, economically, and many aspects of Colombia reminded Glenn of some of his own qualities of administration (even though he long ago dropped the idea of business administration, it was still a part of him, and he liked the idea of people who seemed to be businesslike.)

While much of Latin America fits the picture of huts and villages, Colombia has a distinct industrial and religious personality of its own. To a young man like Glenn with missionary zeal and a frustrated love for the city and the life of commerce, Colombia was a mission field that called forth a deep and fervent response. Very early, both Glenn and I felt a love for this country. We were especially attracted to the city of Bogota.

Next came the paperwork for the Assemblies of God church. There were reams of it. The church requires a life history from all prospective missionaries. For a year there is a series of tests. Medically, is there physical stamina for the work? Psychologically, can the candidates cope with problems in the mission field? Can this couple adapt to the culture shock?

After thorough testing comes a time of speaking to many congregations, in order to raise money needed for support. The hopeful missionary receives a budget that states the amount of money needed for working in a particular country. This amount includes living expenses and funds required for missionary services or other evangelistic endeavors. In the Assemblies of God church, a prospective missionary must raise the budget money in the form of pledges from congregations.

Once pledges in the needed amount are secured, the green light is given to proceed to the next step, which is language study for a year. Only after these goals are accomplished does the denomination grant permission to go to the assigned country as a called missionary.

The testing was done; the first papers completed; the budget prepared. Glenn resigned from the church in Concord, so he and I could give all our time to raising money for a missionary assignment. We went from church to church, sharing our vision and gathering pledges. The Assemblies of God church would discern what type of monthly budget we would need for our four-year assignment in Colombia, plus language school training. We would then have their approval to speak about this financial need in the Assemblies of God churches and ask for pledges that would amount to probably more than two thousand dollars each month.

When the various churches had signed their pledges and the requested budget had been met, we would then begin to prepare for the next step, language training. Finally, after completing the language training, we would go to the country of our calling, Colombia.

AN UNEXPECTED REJECTION

All that remained now was the final approval of the quarterly board meeting from the Assemblies of God. With our furniture in storage in Los Angeles, we waited for the official phone call on the appointed eve. Friends were giving us a small farewell party.

"Glenn," the church official began, "I'm sorry, but there is a problem. I can't tell you why at this moment, but you and Marilynn won't be able to go as missionaries. The board has rejected your request."

After many tears and frantic phone calls, the story emerged. The senior pastor's wife in Concord had sent a letter to the district claiming Glenn and I were unfit for service as missionaries. She had seen us as a young couple working hard to advance what she described as "our own programs." But somehow she had not seen us advancing the programs and pastoral plan of the church as set forth by her husband. Yes, the senior pastor had been busy with his master's degree program and also distracted with illness. But in this woman's opinion, we Kramars were less than devoted stewards to him and his plan for the church.

When servants of the Lord disagree; only God can settle the issue. It matters not who is right or wrong according to evidence that meets the eye or reaches the ear. God looks at the inner evidence of the heart. He is concerned about what type of person the servant will become after a trial. We get distracted about what's happening during the trial.

Out of the darkness, two Scriptures came clearly to my mind and heart. "Vengeance is mine, says the Lord"; and "Be still and know that I am God."

We returned to Los Angeles with broken hearts and asked the Assemblies of God board to reconsider. They told us to wait for six months, after which time the board would reassemble and consider our request. We were two young people totally in their hands. We had a right to ask for consideration, but their answer would be final. They literally held our lives in their hands.

After six months of suspense the board assembled to reconsider their decision.

With officials gathered around a meeting table, the senior pastor defended his wife and restated all the accusations she had made in the letter.

Glenn had been told to say nothing, so he sat silently.

When the pastor finally finished, the superintendent turned to Glenn who was sitting next to him at the table. He shifted in his chair and put one leg across the other knee. After a moment, he nudged Glenn and lifted his foot so Glenn could see the words written on the sole of his shoe, "Apologize to Pastor M. (the senior pastor)."

In his heart, Glenn felt he had nothing to apologize for. But he had done enough soul-searching during these tense weeks to clear his mind. We had both come to realize that Jesus loves Pastor M., and we must too, even if we disagreed.

As Scripture calls us to, esteeming the senior pastor better than himself, Glenn said, "I'm sorry, Pastor M., for any misunderstanding we've ever had and for anything I've done to give you this opinion of us."

Then I walked across the room and put my arms around this beloved adversary. "We love you and always will," I told him sincerely.

Glenn and the senior pastor embraced. Tears were flowing now. And so was the opportunity for us to follow the Lord's direction into South America.

THE CHALLENGE OF LANGUAGE TRAINING

The first stop on the way to our mission field would be language school in Mexico. Here all new missionaries learned to deal with the babel of foreign languages they would soon encounter. A full year was allotted for raising funds to support these studies.

Mark was now four years old. Night after night he would sit through the fund-raising services and had begun to learn his father's sermons. "Mommy," he would say, "Next, Daddy's going to tell them about..." This was no babel to him.

Pledges mounted until at last we had the required amount and could begin final preparations. But now a new problem troubled me.

Mark was born with a weakness in his chest and had severe attacks of asthma. During the year of traveling for the pledges to various church congregations, he had become increasingly worse. Many nights he had such difficulty breathing he would turn blue, and my heart would ache for him. How could we go to Mexico this way? It was one thing to suffer yourself and yet another to see your child gasping for air!

Night after night, as Mark lay in his bed sleeping fitfully, with us beside him in prayer, God assured us that if we were obedient to his direction for our lives, he would take care of Mark's illness. Faith is seeing beyond our sickness and weakness and believing in the promises God has set before us.

On the evening before departure for language school in Guadalajara, Mark had another attack. But as we continued to pray, we knew God would help us if we took the first step toward Mexico and language school. As we drove toward the Mexican border, we knew God had answered our prayers. Mark was breathing normally and never again was there a wheeze from him. Nor has he ever had a problem again with asthma.

For many of the couples at the school, the husband was the one preparing for ministry, while the wife was there to support him and care for their children. It was different in my case. I had a conviction that I had been called into the ministry along with Glenn. Language was part of my

A Search for Direction / 49

preparation to answer that call. So I immersed myself in the study of Spanish.

These classes also included homiletics, the art of writing and preaching sermons. They were offered to men and women alike. Naturally, I took advantage of this opportunity. I enjoyed the challenge of preparing spiritual talks and proclamations. In fact, I liked this door to spiritual service through language so much that I found an extra tutor on the side. Perceiving a talent, he encouraged me in that area. Together we worked for hours on the verbs and nouns I needed to breathe life into a scriptural proclamation.

These were very happy days for Kim and Mark, Glenn and me. The language school offered nursery school and grammar school for the children, so each morning we were off as a family for a day at school. Each afternoon while Glenn and I studied, the kids found new playmates in the neighborhood. Within a matter of weeks, they were even speaking Spanish without ever studying the language at all.

I was blessed with a live-in maid who helped me with everything.

Every weekend we took advantage of the beautiful surroundings and planned a short trip to one of the tourist places of Mexico. Barra De Navidad was our favorite beach. This was a small fishing town on the Pacific coast where Mark learned to swim in the warm ocean waters. There we would happily sit on the beach, peeling shrimp as the fishermen's boats passed nearby.

Along with our associates from the Assemblies of God, there were missionaries at the language school from many other Protestant churches. I had never been intimately involved with any but our own. Working side by side with people of other denominations who shared our zeal for the Lord was a new but important experience in my global calling.

We became very much a part of the other missionaries' lives. Some of our best friends were from the Wycliffe Bible

Translators. We were excited to share with them the baptism in the Spirit.

Some of the missionaries came from historic Protestant backgrounds and were becoming curious about the charismatic dimensions of spirituality. We were well accepted by them all. That year of language training will always be a highlight in my life.

While I forged ahead, Glenn struggled. Class work and language were not his forte. The desire was there; the effort was there; but something else was happening in his life.

DELIVERANCE FROM ILLNESS

Every so often in life an event occurs that burns itself into your memory. Not only does it seem intense at the time, but also it stands out, even while it is happening, as something you'll always remember. This was one of those occasions.

"Name?" inquired the nurse in Spanish.

"Kramar. Glenn Kramar," I answered.

"Oh, God, what's wrong with him?" I wondered. He looked so sick.

I clung to the wheelchair they had brought for Glenn. My own legs were weak, and I wondered whether it was fear for Glenn or something else. The lights in the admitting room seemed so bright. My eyes ached and my head throbbed.

"Age?"

"Thirty." Why didn't they just take him in and put him to bed without all these questions? "Oh, God! Take care of Glenn."

Thoughts, questions, and prayers swirled in my mind. My body ached deep inside, and I began to fear that whatever condition Glenn had contracted was starting in me.

"We'll take good care of him, and we'll be speaking with you as soon as possible," the nurse said, and she wheeled Glenn off to a room.

I walked dazedly out to the car, feeling more and more faint. I had to get back to the children. I was in the midst of preparing to go back to Los Angeles. There was so much to be done. Plans were being made to leave for Colombia soon after we returned to California. But with both of us sick, how could that be done? If I were to become as sick as Glenn, who would care for the children or even take all of us back to the States?

I climbed into the car, laid my head on the steering wheel and called out in desperation, "God, I can't make it. Please take away this sickness."

Immediately, the response came into my heart and mind. "There is nothing to fear. You will be all right. Go on home."

Instantly, I felt the healing begin, cooling my aching body and quieting my throbbing head. There swelled up within me a growing sense of well-being and hope.

I drove home with renewed strength. There I completed the packing, loaded the car, helped the children, and attended to all the affairs of leaving the school at Guadalajara.

However, despite the fact I had been healed, there was still a problem with Glenn. His illness had been diagnosed as hepatitis, a sickness common in Mexico, and there was nothing they could do to cure him.

He was released to the apartment, but did not improve. Soon the return to California could be put off no longer.

We climbed into the car with the children in back. I was driving, and Glenn sat there beside me. He was so uncomfortable I soon realized that he would never make it north unless God intervened.

I knew that God's eyes were on us and that he would answer my call for help. But I didn't know when or how.

Deliverance came dramatically after one difficult encampment on the beach at Mazatlán. Glenn lay down that evening with terrible fits of pain and discomfort. The next morning he got up feeling much the same. But for some unexplainable reason he sat behind the wheel of the car and said, "I'm driving home." Every mile of the way, I asked, "How are you feeling?" and each time the answer was, "I'm better." By the time we drove into Los Angeles, he was so much better that he could walk normally and feel new strength. In the sunny bedroom of my parents home, Glenn finished recuperating and felt well enough to go to Colombia.

Times like these reassured me that God would never leave me nor forsake me. Even today, I look back on those special times for renewed faith and courage.

HOLY FAITH CROSSES THE PACIFIC

The Grace Line ship, the Sante Fe, throbbed impatiently in her berth in Long beach harbor. It was early evening and already beyond the scheduled departure time. Darkness was beginning to fall. This cargo ship would carry only ten passengers, among them Glenn and me, Mark, age five, and tiny Kim, age three.

For thousands of years Christian missionaries have been sailing away on the open seas to spread the gospel, but as far as we were concerned, we were the first.

The ship's hands had been off on port leave and returned to the vessel intoxicated. As the Sante Fe began to move away, our crowd of loved ones and well wishers below sang out the haunting strains of "Amazing Grace." Some of the sailors staggered to the rails and woozily joined the singing. It was at this moment that I took great reassurance in the fact that the name of our ship, *Sante Fe,* meant "Holy Faith" in Spanish. Judging from such a departure, we would need extra faith at every turn.

As the Sante Fe slipped quietly across the evening waters, I felt the excitement of departure engulfed by darkness and loneliness. Gone was the security of family, friends, and native land. Ahead lay untold hardships and wonder. It helped a little when I faintly heard Kim singing to the captain, "My boat is so little, the ocean so wide. But Jesus is holding my hand."

Quickly, I redirected my thoughts to the bright and warm words of encouragement my parents had spoken in the last few days. My father, Pastor Roberts, had recounted promises from the Good Shepherd to guide his flock.

Mother's parting words were simpler but more perplexing. That previous evening in Long Beach a prophecy came to her mind. "You will have many children in Israel." These were puzzling words. Was I going to have a larger family? Were we going to the Holy Land? Many years later I came to understand how God fulfilled that word through the ministry he has given me.

Seeing my parents at the dock—my father's strong hand waving—broke my heart. All I knew about my missionary call was not enough to calm the sadness in my soul. I cried with everything within me.

I heard Mark's little voice calling from the deck, "Grandma, Grandpa, I love you." And he kept calling to them until we could see them no longer. It seemed as if those of us on the boat and those on the docks were dying again to ourselves for God's purposes to be completed in us.

Fortunately, the trip was wonderful. We stopped at every port on the way to Colombia. Mark and Kim made friends with all of the sailors. We even discovered the captain's wife was herself an evangelist back home.

One event in Mark's shipboard life was a minor miracle. Fishing off the deck was naturally a great pastime. One day Glenn asked Mark, "What kind of fish would you like to catch the most?"

"A shark," came the quick and positive reply.

"Why a shark? That could be a lot of trouble. And what would we do with it after you caught it?"

"I dunno, but I wanna catch a shark," persisted the impressionable boy.

"Well, Mark," said his dad kneeling down to eye level. "If

you ask Jesus in faith, he has promised to give you the desires of your heart. Maybe we could pray together and God would let you catch a shark."

"Really?" bubbled Mark in anticipation.

After a short prayer to heaven, Mark committed his hook to the sea. Almost immediately something struck the line with intensity.

"Hang on. Pull it in," shouted Glenn.

In a few short moments, which most likely seemed like the three-year hunt for Moby Dick to Mark, up came a bellicose fish about the size of a small dog.

"It's a shark all right," declared one of the sailors. "A small one."

"What about that?" Glenn said. Mark was beaming from ear to ear. "See what can happen when you ask Jesus for the desires of your heart?"

"Yeah," he exclaimed with boyish enthusiasm.

Later in life this experience with faith would help prepare Mark to deal with the sharks of temptation that would prowl his own harbors.

GETTING SETTLED IN COLOMBIA

The Sante Fe deposited her faith-filled passengers on Colombian shores on March 1, 1966. Opportunities came fast and furious in Bogota. Not only his preaching in the many storefront churches of the Assemblies of God, but also Glenn's administrative abilities were immediately recognized by all. Within days Glenn was named as administrator for the Bible school. Within four weeks he was teaching seven major classes. By July 1, he was named counselor for the eighteen Assemblies of God churches in the capital city of Bogota.

Everything we touched turned to gold, it seemed. It was as if God were opening the windows of heaven to compensate us for all the closed doors we had encountered in the last two years getting here.

Even our children found new friends in Bogota's American school. We had a new live-in maid to help us at home. Mark seemed quite proud as he put on his new school uniform each day, and his dad would comb his hair and send him off to catch the school bus that picked up him and his sister in front of our rented home.

Soon our household furnishings had been unpacked and our new home was in reasonably good shape. We had brought many things with us from the United States to make it feel like home, and life became a new adventure and a real joy. The kids soon discovered the sorts of toys that were made and sold in the city and realized that even a simpler way of life could be exciting.

Soon the interdenominational projects called Evangelism in Depth were brought to our attention. A large crusade involving all the Protestant missions was planned for the city. Glenn was needed to promote the crusade on radio and television, and the organizers decided that I should play piano and lead the choirs for this event. I remember praying that this opportunity might unlock my world beyond the limits of the piano's eighty-eight keys.

The crusade was led by Evangelist Paul Finkenbinder, and Glenn developed a beautiful closeness with him and many other missionaries in the various Protestant churches.

Officials from the Assemblies of God church were not enthralled by our attention to other friends in these interdenominational crusades. But still they respected us enough to endorse us for a unique honor.

THE CALL TO LEADERSHIP

The church constitution requires that the superintendent for the entire country have a minimum of one year's experience in that country. We had been there only a matter of months. But local church leaders felt we were the ones best qualified to fill the post, even though some other missionaries had eighteen or twenty years' seniority.

Much to our surprise, the national convention amended their constitution and elected Glenn as superintendent with a unanimous vote.

I was elected to head the women's activities. My responsibility was to oversee projects and raise money for supporting pastors and their families in all fifty organized churches and two hundred missions in the country.

Where to start? How to proceed?

We also felt that our children needed to be with us as we traveled, especially on weekends. As we visited the churches, they would accompany us. We often stopped as a family to enjoy this beautiful country. I remember the times we stopped to swim in the rivers. Then there were times the kids encouraged us to stop along the roadsides to buy *arepas* (the Colombian tortilla) and also *marzorca* (corn on the cob).

As new missionaries and new arrivals to Colombia, we had a voracious appetite for answers to all kinds of questions. Fortunately, the superintendent's office was led by a grand chef of resourcefulness, Esther Garzón.

Esther was a young girl with grown-up problems. During our first months in Colombia, both of her parents had died, leaving Esther responsible for ten brothers and sisters. Soon she discovered she had a gift for work and organization. With it she not only cared for the large family, but brought a measure of brilliance to the superintendent's office.

With her down-to-earth approach to practical matters, knowledge of the nation, and love for God, Esther helped us work miracles for the local pastors. She taught Glenn to speak with the tongues of men and of angels in Spanish. She helped me understand all mysteries behind the people and customs of Colombia. She gave Mark and Kim as much love as her own family. As a team for Jesus, we appeared to move mountains.

While Glenn was out working with the pastors, I addressed myself to the needs of their wives and families. In addition to practical matters regarding nutrition and child rearing, I struggled to develop spiritual messages in Spanish. One of my first "sermons" came from the Twenty-Third Psalm. Despite the fact that the main text was written in six verses, I spent hours working on the proper Spanish to help the message jump off the page in a personal way for my audience. As Esther listened with patience, she gave me the courage to try.

We grew to love this young woman as a real sister in the Lord. Such strong bonds in the Spirit would later prove life-saving when other bonds in the flesh were beginning to decay.

Were we *really* prepared, though, for the challenges that lay ahead in this predominantly Catholic country? Time would tell.

THREE

Challenges in Colombia

SOON AFTER ARRIVING in Colombia, something happened to Glenn that gave us both cause for alarm. It also steered us toward a new direction that would ultimately change our lives.

POLITICAL AND RELIGIOUS UPHEAVAL
IN AN UNSTABLE COUNTRY

While progressive economically, we soon learned Colombia was also a country of violence, political upheaval, and revolution. The political situation was especially unstable during the first months of our time in Colombia. A particular law, "La Reforma Agraria," which affected the farmers and agricultural workers, was beginning to be enforced. This meant that the rights of the farm workers were at stake, so the revolutionaries began to fight against the government in order to demand the rights of the farm workers. Such fighting caused much confusion and strife, especially in the outlying towns and villages.

Even though this strife (and many times violence) had been going on for at least twelve years, it seemed to settle down somewhat during the first months of our time in Colombia. But the memories and heartbreak of these years were still confronting the people. They were sensitive and easily stirred up.

Also at this time, evangelical churches started coming into Colombia in great numbers, often confusing and worsening the relationships between the Catholic church and other denominations. Since Colombia was 99 percent Catholic, this caused great division, mistrust, and religious persecution.

NEARLY STONED BY THE CATHOLICS

Not long after receiving his appointment as superintendent of the country, Glenn and three associates climbed into his red, four-year-old Fiat for a visit to one of the mountain missionary posts at Cogua. There the new converts believed their lives were in danger. They had been threatened by the local Catholics.

Glenn pulled into the village. His passengers, two leaders from the Cogua congregation and one fellow worker from Bogota, stepped out with him and walked down the street toward the house where the meetings were being held. Glenn tried to reassure them. "These villagers won't do the violent things you're expecting."

The villagers looked friendly enough and seemed to be going about their daily business. But it was hard to ignore the ominous stones piled at intervals along the walkways.

Upon reaching the group of many converts, who filled the small frame home of the new believers, Glenn reminded them, "The Lord is with us." He gathered the small group of men, women, and children into an open patio to pray.

"Lord Jesus, we thank you for being in our midst. Though we . . ."

Suddenly there was a loud thud. Rocks began sailing into

the side of the house. Several flew across the open patio. A child cried out in pain, and blood ran from his cheek. Although he wasn't seriously hurt, the men knew he might have been. They had to leave so the barrage would stop.

"Evangelicals! Get out! We don't want you here!" The shouts were coming from outside the patio wall. Someone pounded at the door.

"We'll be leaving," one of the evangelicals shouted to the mob, which was led by the local priest. Quickly, the men prayed and laid hands on those within the house and asked for protection for them. Then, saying a prayer for their own protection, Glenn and the others with him left the house quickly and ran for the car.

The angry villagers turned their attack from the house and followed the men, who were now running for their lives. With a last desperate effort they reached the Fiat, gunned it and headed out of the city with rocks following close behind.

As the three other men in the car heatedly debated what action should be taken against their attackers, Glenn tried to cling to God's promise: "all things work together for good for those who love God and are called according to his purpose" (Rom 8:28).

Though the men in the car urged reprisal and his own thoughts surged within him, Glenn began to hear another, quieter voice urging a course of action entirely untried. This approach would not only turn the tide of sentiment in favor of the Christians in Cogua and others throughout Colombia, but it would ultimately help lead Glenn and me toward a new flock in the Lord.

"Where's the nearest Catholic bishop?"

"Zipaquira," came the reply. "Why?"

"Because we need to pay this gentleman a visit."

Upon arriving, Glenn was surprised by the haste with which his request for an audience was answered. Soon he found himself face-to-face with the bishop who was a giant of a man. As Glenn approached, the bishop extended his hand for the customary kiss of a bishop's ring. Glenn responded with a handshake.

Feeling much like Daniel before the pagan king of Babylon, Glenn explained the situation and asked for assurances of safety. He was prepared for hostility or polite inaction, but not the reply that followed.

"It's not my desire that these things be done," countered the bishop. "I give you my assurance there will be no more incidents of this nature."

And so it happened. Our Colombian believers went back to Cogua and continued working on behalf of the Assemblies of God.

Unimpressive as this encounter was, it set the precedent for numerous contacts to follow. Where other members of the Assemblies of God felt that retribution was justified, Glenn and I felt that reconciliation was possible. It almost appeared these men of the Catholic church respected the will of the same Jesus we did.

Still the hot-blooded nature of the local Colombians was not to be denied. Other conflagrations ignited. Zealots attacked another missionary outpost, this time using fire bombs. Fortunately no one was seriously injured, but the local Assemblies of God pastors shouted for retribution and government protection.

"No, God has shown us another way," we insisted. Glenn went straight to the responsible Catholic authority, Archbishop Ocampo.

AN UNLIKELY ALLIANCE

Again the reception was sympathetic. Once past the cordialities which included a cup of steaming Colombian coffee, Glenn reassured the archbishop about his intentions in the country. "Our work is to bring the gospel to those

Challenges in Colombia / 63

who do not know Jesus. I understand that 99 percent of the people in Colombia are baptized Roman Catholics, but only 17 percent, by the statistics of the bishops, go to Mass once a year or more. We aren't after that 17 percent. We want to reach the 83 percent who don't go to church, those who are alienated from the church."

"Someone must reach these people with the gospel. The people here are badly in need of spiritual help. Our country is wounded. Colombia is in need a great deal of healing and reconciliation," the archbishop responded, to Glenn's amazement.

Glenn detailed for the archbishop what had taken place, assuring him it was not hearsay, but an authentic case. The archbishop listened sympathetically.

"Archbishop, could we do something together to publicly reverse this?" he asked.

"This is not in the spirit of Vatican II," Archbishop Ocampo said fervently, referring to an event Glenn had, to that moment, not heard about but of which he was to become increasingly aware.

Next the archbishop surprised Glenn even more. He suggested they pray together about the situation. Pray together! A Jesuit and an Assemblies of God preacher!

As they lifted up their voices in unison and shared the Word of God in Scripture, Glenn suddenly knew that their hearts were one. They were brothers in Christ!

A wave of gratitude and praise flooded over Glenn as the realization came to him. It was the devil himself he expected to see, not a Jesuit Christian. But the archbishop's goals and aims were his own goals and aims. The older man wanted a living faith for his people. Though there were many things Glenn did not understand, he knew this prayer came from a union of spirits. Upon departure, the archbishop enclosed him in a warm Colombian *abrazo* (embrace), and Glenn knew he was embracing his brother.

"You really prayed together?" I remember asking incredulously when Glenn shared his experience a few hours later. "How can you pray with a Catholic? They're not Christians. Catholics are not part of the body of Christ."

"When we prayed, Marilynn, I knew he was my brother. I don't understand it either, but I know it's true," replied Glenn.

In the months that followed, Glenn spoke to many bishops and priests throughout Colombia whenever and wherever there was an outbreak of violence. It was some time before we understood exactly what was behind "Vatican II." But we knew immediately that if it was opposed to violence, we were in favor of it.

Among other things, Vatican II called for reconciliation and peace in the body of Christ. In the Vatican II document on ecumenism, Catholics are invited to take what is right and good in the Lord from brothers and sisters of other Christian traditions and allow those experiences to become areas of newfound unity and collaboration in the body of Christ.

In fact, this document presents a compelling charge:

> ... Catholics must joyfully acknowledge and esteem the truly Christian endowments from our common heritage which are to be found among our separated brethren. It is right and salutary to recognize the riches of Christ and virtuous works in the lives of others who are bearing witness to Christ, sometimes even to the shedding of their blood. For God is always wonderful in his works and worthy of admiration. Nor should we forget that whatever is wrought by the grace of the Holy Spirit in the hearts of our separated brethren can contribute to our own edification. Whatever is truly Christian never conflicts with the genuine interest of the faith; indeed, it can always bring a more ample realization of the very mystery of Christ and the Church. **Decree on Ecumenism, ch. 1, no. 4**

Glenn began to remind some of the village priests that what was happening was not in the spirit of this new understanding, quietly trusting they would comprehend, even though he did not always comprehend.

It mattered not who was right or wrong. The important thing was to admit mistakes. The natural tendency of the Protestant and Pentecostal pastors was to fight for their rights. They found it difficult to believe that a person with an open heart could go to a Catholic and ask God to forgive and to heal.

But God has promised, "If my people, who are called by my name, will humble themselves and pray and seek my face and turn from their wicked ways, then I will hear from heaven and will forgive their sin and heal their land" (2 Chr 7:14). Could it be these Catholics were "my people" as well?

TV APPEARANCE WITH FR. HERREROS

One priest in Bogota proved especially helpful. Fr. Garcia Herreros was founder of a social reform group known as *El Minuto de Dios*, "The Minute of God." Fr. Herreros had for many years worked to help construct new housing for the working-class people. He also raised money to educate and give job training to young people. He gave aid to disaster areas and was known as the forerunner of social reform in the country.

Fr. Herreros was the only one allowed on national TV for religious communication. After hearing of our first experiences of harassment and the problems we had confronted, and then of our desire to work for reconciliation and peace in Colombia, he took an immediate liking to us and offered to help. In fact, Fr. Herreros was brave enough to include a Baptist pastor in his own youth ministry long before the advent of Vatican II. What he offered to do for us was even more dramatic.

"Would you like to go on television with me and proclaim together?" he asked us.

Naturally, Glenn took him up on the invitation. Fr.

Herreros became not only a personal ally in our struggle for unity, but a personal friend as well.

Day after day, Glenn came home telling about the wondrous ways in which God was answering our prayers in our relationships with Catholics.

"You won't believe this, Marilynn," he would start off. Then he would share how God had resolved problems in response to our humble attitude and willingness to approach the Catholic priests. Even other missionaries could hardly believe what was happening.

Priests came to ask forgiveness, and the Protestant or Pentecostal pastors granted it. Because of the reconciliation taking place, pastors who, in the past, had been unable to purchase food or clothing for their families, could walk among the people without fear. This miracle of peace came to village after village.

A VISION OF A CHALICE

About this time a mysterious vision appeared to us. We were both in prayer at the same time in different parts of the house when the same vision came upon us.

"Honey, it was as though I saw an altar with a chalice being raised over all the people," I related to Glenn.

"Yes, and I think I know what happened next," interrupted Glenn. "The church was filled with people praising the Lord, around the altar and around the Body and Blood of Jesus."

This brought a chill to my spine. "Then you saw it too!" I exclaimed. "What does it all mean?"

The answer would not emerge in its totality for years to come. But this mutual vision gave us an immediate sense of confidence and joy about our work in and around so many fervent Catholics.

A VISIT TO CARTAGENA

By this time we were committed to working ourselves out of a job. As superintendent, Glenn had encouraged the Colombian nationals within the church to take over more and more leadership responsibility.

The usual course of missionary work had been to establish a network of churches and missions and bring the converts in, where they would not only be converted to Jesus, but to the missionaries' culture as well. But no one understands the many subtle shades of a national's life and culture without being one. We offered leadership that enabled the Colombian nationals to take over responsibility for their own local churches. This meant training national leaders and helping them adopt their own policies according to the dictates of the Holy Spirit for their own country. We were the last American superintendents for the Assemblies of God in Colombia.

In August of 1970, having completed two-and-a-half years of our four-year commitment, we decided we needed a break. We filled the Fiat with beach gear—swimming accessories and fishing tackle—and set off with the family for the northern city of Cartagena and a vacation in the Caribbean sun.

Cartagena, a city of four hundred thousand people, is the most fortified city in all of Latin America. Some four hundred years ago, the Spanish built their forts there to hide gold and jewels. All over the city, large forts rise like miniature mountains.

These forts were constructed with the tears, blood, and sweat of first, the Colombian natives, who were brought down from the interior mountains as slaves, and then by blacks from Africa. Accustomed to the high country, the Colombian natives were unable to survive the intense heat and humidity of the coastal area for more than three months.

African slaves were much hardier: they lasted about six months.

Christianity here was popularized by a Jesuit missionary named Peter Claver, who later became a saint in the Catholic church. He went as a missionary to the slaves, and when he found them dying, he organized hospitals to care for them as they succumbed under the cruel labor. Through Peter Claver's ministry, thousands of these slaves were converted to Christ.

Cartagena was so different from Bogota as to seem, for all practical purposes, a different country. Where the Bogotans were conservative, the Cartagenans were a vibrant, open people. Their city reminded us of Jamaica. Eighty-five percent of them were black. The lifestyle was that of a tropical city with a lusty rhythm, even open sex.

And there was the Caribbean Sea. Glenn and I enjoyed the city for its historical interest, but our born-and-bred love for California's hot sand and cool sea breezes found its fulfillment in the exquisite beaches of Cartagena and the waters of the Caribbean.

"I have the strangest feeling we're supposed to return to Cartagena," I told Glenn one day during that visit.

But the thought seemed practically absurd. We had a phenomenally successful ministry in Bogota. Besides our position with the Assemblies of God, there were the interdenominational projects, the crusades, and the radio and television broadcasts. For some time Glenn had served as treasurer for the joint efforts of all the Protestant missionary groups in Colombia.

With the grace of God and the help of many others, we had made some giant strides back in Bogota. Where only a few years before, the plaza or townsquare in Colombia's cities had been the scene of a bloody revolution and people from different churches dying at the hands of other Christians, now there was a spiritual revolution of genuine brotherhood and revival. Fellow Christians marched down the streets of the city not with weapons, but with Bibles, singing hymns to God. It was a glorious time and we were happy to be a part of it.

Further, we had only eighteen months left on this commitment in Colombia. What could we possibly accomplish in this huge city of Cartagena with its rampant vice in so short a time?

But still the urge persisted and grew.

There were no Assemblies of God activities in Cartagena, only a few mission boards that had worked there unsuccessfully for the most part. The Catholic church had, of course, been there for centuries, but few people attended. Only about 3 to 5 percent of the people of Cartagena attended church at all, and these were mostly women and children. The rest had virtually no active faith, hoping that being baptized, married, and buried in the church would somehow assure them a place in heaven.

Cartagena was not, in the natural sense, a promising mission field—especially for two young, city-oriented missionaries tuned to administrative work, with only a few months to plant, cultivate, and harvest.

Still, there was that pull on the heart—"Come back to Cartagena." By this time I had come to realize the hand that was drawing the strings, and I dared not resist.

A NEW CHALLENGE: THE CALL TO CARTAGENA

Though we had gone to Cartagena only to rest in the sun for a few days and enjoy the seashore, we prepared to return to whatever challenge God had waiting for us in that teeming city.

This wasn't a popular decision among the other missionaries, who reminded us of the practical realities. There were also mixed feelings about turning the administration of the Assemblies of God over to national Colombians.

But God knows how to take care of his own. Within a matter of months, the Colombians elected, for the first time, a leader of national descent as their superintendent. Now we were free to go.

But where would we go? Where would we start?

"Remember Padricka?" I asked Glenn.

Padricka was a small black lady who sold cold drinks and candies at one of the forts which was now a tourist attraction in Cartagena. Her beautiful little girl of four had caught the eye of our whole family.

"Let's go see her," I encouraged.

We found Padricka still there among the throngs selling her confectioneries. "Marilynn! Glenn!" She reached across the flimsy counter and hugged us excitedly.

"But where's your little girl, Padricka?" we asked.

Tears filled the black eyes. "My daughter is very sick. She has a terrible disease." Then, in a voice that betrayed a faint hope, she asked, almost apologetically, "Do you think you could pray for her?"

"Of course, Padricka. Where is she?" answered Glenn.

Padricka lived in San Francisco, a barrio outside Cartagena. *San Francisco* is Spanish for St. Francis. St. Francis of Assisi was a saint from thirteenth century Italy, who espoused a life of simplicity and poverty. Never was a community more aptly named. Five thousand people had been displaced from a slum area to make room for a highway and had been given land in this area with the promise of possession if they built a home. So the people put up shacks made of paper, palm branches, or whatever they could find—anything to call a shelter. There were no sewage facilities other than open pits in the ground. There were no sidewalks and no semblance of order. There were not even any house numbers because there were no formal streets.

It was here that we found Padricka's sick child. Since we came later on our own, we had to go from shack to shack asking, "Do you know of a woman named Padricka?"

Crowds of the curious peered at us, wondering who these Americans were and why they were here. Naked or nearly so, black children followed, some shyly, some laughing and teasing.

Finally, we found Padricka. As we prepared to pray over the little girl, many of the people gathered around. As they listened, they too began to pray in their own simple ways. Most of these people had been baptized but had never attended Mass. Most did not know anything about God except the bare facts that he existed, and he had left behind a church whose priests were to lead them to heaven. They knew little more of the faith whose name they claimed.

After praying, Glenn stayed and talked to the mother and her friends. Meanwhile, I walked out into the street. Immediately, I was surrounded by what appeared to be a tribe of small Africans—tiny, ragged or naked children with silky, ebony skin. They bombarded me with questions and excited conversation.

"Do you know Jesus?" I asked them in turn. "Do you know who he is?"

All they could do was look up at me with bewilderment. They didn't know how to answer.

"Do you know about the one who was nailed to a cross so you could go to heaven?" I persisted. Again, they seemed to have no idea of how much they were loved.

My heart melted. Suddenly, there came in the midst of the heat and the flies and the clamor of the children, a clear, sweet voice speaking again: "You're to come back here and start your first church."

When Glenn stepped outside to join me I said to him, "I think we're supposed to come back here."

"I've already talked to Padricka," Glenn answered. "We can use her house and neighbors will come for meetings."

So this was it! The first church we had expected to begin so long ago and far away in affluent, suburban Danville, California, was instead to be here in the barrio of San

Francisco, Cartagena in Colombia, among the poorest of the poor.

The joy of the Lord was overwhelming. Rich people, poor people mattered not at all. What was important was preaching the life and teaching of Jesus.

WERE WE "CRAZY" TO GO TO SAN FRANCISCO?

Only 5 percent of the people in that part of Cartagena had a home life with a father. The rest of them lived a life totally devoid of normal structures and strictures.

Many of the women became prostitutes at an early age without even thinking about it. They simply shared their bodies in return for what they needed. Everything belonged to everybody as people moved freely from one shack to another. Most of the teenage boys were *marijuaneros*, smoking and pushing.

"You're crazy," exclaimed a horrified friend back in Cartagena. "Don't go back there."

"Why not?" I asked, puzzled.

"Because they'll pull a knife and kill you. They think nothing of it."

"She's right," the friend's husband agreed. "I'm the head of social work in Cartagena, and there's no hope for San Francisco. People have to be controlled by the police. The Peace Corps has come and gone. Aid for them has been offered and not accepted. All the national and social organizations have given up there."

"We refuse to believe there's no hope," we insisted, remembering the simple prayers of Padricka over her sick child. "Their need is desperate, and God came in the flesh to help such as these."

"These people are like animals," the friend insisted. "They are like a wild tribe, and no one can help them. If you try to do anything for them, they beat it all down. The Peace Corps built a small center for them. People came to teach them handicrafts so they could have money to live, but those savages took sticks and beat the center down. No," he said shaking his head with finality and regret, "don't think you can do anything in San Francisco. It's impossible."

"Give us six months here and we'll show you what God can do," Glenn said. "Even though man can't do it, God can."

"Then for God's sake," the friend pleaded, "go alone. Don't let Marilynn go, and don't go into that place at night. The marijuaneros will kill and rape and think nothing of it."

But the call was there. I knew God had not intended for Glenn to work alone. And night services were necessary. So we left the children in the care of a maid when I had to go at night and committed them to God—knowing there was danger, but that God was over all.

"Jesus, you asked me to work with these little children, so I leave my own children in your care. I trust you." That was my prayer.

So I kissed them and hugged their firm, healthy little bodies to my own and went out to minister to other little ones who had nothing but dirt under their feet. We brought virtually nothing of material value to share with them, but we knew we had to give them what we could: a knowledge that Jesus loved them. We prayed that would be enough.

Glenn sold the Fiat and bought an old 1943 Dodge pickup truck with a large blue-and-white canopy covering the back. Beneath the canopy were benches. With Glenn at the wheel, we chugged into San Francisco, picking up children as we went. Children from everywhere jumped on for the ride to the meeting, and the whole unlikely crowd plowed through the dirt streets, screaming, singing, and laughing. This ritual came to be a regular occurrence.

Kim has told me that hearing of these outings are some of her earliest memories as a child.

From the first meetings at Padricka's house, other

meetings sprang up, for people became eager to have their own humble houses visited. And Padricka's little girl, whose illness had been epilepsy, started to get well. She began to live a normal life.

A few people with cement block houses offered their larger and more secure living rooms for our meetings. The crowds of children had now grown to three or four hundred, so I stood with my accordion in the streets with the children, while Glenn led the meetings inside. Often we would literally pick men up off the ground were they had fallen in a drunken stupor from too much *agua ardiente* (ardent water), and carry them inside. We would pray over them and ask the Lord to revive them enough, so they could develop an ardor for Jesus.

"Lord, I don't know what to do with these kids," I prayed. But there they were, hundreds of them, waiting, and I knew I had to do something with them. So I taught them the simple little choruses I had grown up with. When they became quiet, I told them short stories of Jesus.

Back home in Cartagena, we gathered small bits of paper and pictures. Mark and Kim helped me prepare hundreds of Scripture verses and Bible pictures for the children.

JOHNNY MEETS JESUS

Night after night, I noticed a slim teenage boy. He always stood over to the side, watching. His large, liquid eyes would steadily gaze out of his flawless, black face with an expression so candid and filled with such a hunger for life and beauty that my heart ached.

"Johnny's a marijuanero," one of the younger children told me one day. "You'd better watch out for him." The other little children agreed that I should be careful of Johnny. But Johnny only stood and watched. He was always there.

"Hey, Johnny," I called to him one night. "Why don't you

come over and help me organize games for the kids?"

Shyly, he came and helped me entertain the little ones. The next night he came back with some of his marijuanero friends to help. We played "Cat and the Rat" and all the games I could remember and others the kids taught me.

When it rained, the games continued in the mud. After several hours of playing, the children would become quiet and gather around for Bible stories and more songs.

I began to go out in the daytime and gather the mothers together and teach them personal hygiene—things I had never learned from a book but which I could see would bring more order into their lives. After these lessons, there would be a Bible class.

Johnny was still there watching. One day I turned to him and said, "Why don't you get all your friends together, and we'll start something for the teenagers, too." By that time, Glenn had taught several women in our Bible study group how to teach the young children. I was free to concentrate on the teenagers.

On the night of the first meeting, Johnny stood waiting as our old Dodge truck lurched its way through the rutted streets, canopy flying, kids screaming with delight. Turning the little ones over to others, I went with Johnny to his friends. Dozens of youngsters, many of whom I had not met, were crammed into the little house. I knew most of them were marijuaneros. Wondering how to start, I picked up the accordion and began speaking to these youngsters in the language they knew best, music.

These children melted my heart. They were so wise in the ways of their small, disordered world, yet so innocent in their need for protection and care.

The song I sang was "The Captain of My Life is Jesus." As the last note died, there was silence, and the presence of Jesus.

"Do you want Jesus to be the captain of your life?" I asked, almost in a whisper.

"Yes," came a reply in a soft, young voice. It was Johnny. "I believe what you say about Jesus, and I want him to be the captain of my life." Then, turning to the other kids, he continued, "I'm going to give my heart to Jesus. Do you want to come with me?"

They began to gather around, their arms holding each other and the tears flowing—these boys who had known nothing of beauty in their lives, and these girls who had given themselves in prostitution since they were twelve or thirteen.

Johnny said, in his own way, the other things he had heard me say: "Lord Jesus, I've done many things that were wrong. I'm a sinner." From the huddled group of youngsters came the echo of his words, as each made a personal admission. "But I ask you to forgive my sins and make me clean." Again, they followed his leading. "I want you to come into my heart, and I will follow you."

"Thank you, Jesus," I whispered through the tears. There was something special about this small group of youngsters saying the words that brought them into the kingdom of peace in God. I remembered the night, when as a youngster like them, I first said yes to Jesus. I felt like saying: "Thank you, Lord, for the disappointments, the illnesses, and the loneliness it took to bring me here." I was overwhelmed with love for these young people. Here were kids who were supposed to knife me in the back. Instead, they had been cut to the bone by the Word of God.

OUR CRITICS ARE PROVEN WRONG: SAN FRANCISCO BECOMES A BEACON OF LIGHT

After that night, the revolution in San Francisco became a hot topic of conversation in the city of Cartagena. It was as if the dark, hidden area that had been a hard core of evil had become a beacon of light to the city, drawing many to come and see what was happening.

Social workers, who had long ago given up hope for San Francisco, became excited. My friend, the same learned doctor who tried to talk me out of working in San Francisco, asked to go with us one night into the barrio. He wanted to see for himself the joy these people who earned less than thirty cents a day could express for the streets of gold in heaven.

We had been told this could not be. "You first have to fill their stomachs." But we had nothing—no food with which to feed their physical bodies. All we had was hope to share. Like Peter and John at the Beautiful Gate in Jerusalem, we had neither silver nor gold, but in the name of Jesus, we told the people to rise and walk (Acts 3:1-6). Now hundreds from the little community of San Francisco were walking in the new life of Jesus.

This was our first church.

Glenn and I went on to establish four churches for the Assemblies of God in Cartagena in little more than two-and-one-half years. The church in San Francisco became self-supporting with its own local pastor.

NEW FRIENDSHIPS DEVELOP

During this time of planting, cultivation, and harvest in San Francisco, Jesus began to introduce a new cutting to my spiritual branches. Across the street from our home in Cartagena was a convent of Carmelite Missionary Sisters (different from the contemplative branch of the order). I couldn't help but notice them as we dashed in and out on our way to San Francisco.

These women were extremely different. They wore a full habit that included veils covering most of the face, even in the most stifling heat. However, even the small portion of countenance that showed through the covering carried a large impact. I couldn't help but notice the nuns' enthusiasm and joy for their role as teachers and nurses. They always said, "Hello," and seemed particularly interested in Mark and Kim.

One day one of the sisters invited me over to the convent as a neighborly gesture. I was glad to accept and found myself doing what any normal Pentecostal missionary would do: I tried to convert them. Not all at once or there on the first visit. But in my heart I knew we had come to Colombia to "win people to Jesus." It didn't occur to me that these nationals might already be his trophy.

Mother Superior was interested in a different aspect of my talent. She wanted to receive accordion lessons.

During that first visit, I was captivated by their liturgy of prayers. The nuns were gathered together to pray, recite the Psalms, and sing. There weren't any chairs, only a ring of pillows neatly arranged on the floor.

"Sit down and join us," said Sr. Magdalena graciously. "We would love to have you play us some music."

I had no trouble understanding the Psalms and their prayers, so I cautiously joined in. What I did have trouble understanding was the easy manner in which the entire convent took me into their hearts as if I were one of their own.

Two of the Carmelites were about my age—in their early thirties. Over the next few days and weeks, we struck up a fast friendship. They became curious about me and wanted to see what I did to work such miracles at San Francisco.

The most natural thing to do was to bring them along. While I was singing or preaching to the children, several of the sisters went door to door visiting families and offering help in personal hygiene and related issues.

"Glenn, it's one of the most wonderful miracles," I remember telling him in one of our many conversations about these godly neighbors. "They seem to have the same love and concern as we do for serving the people in San Francisco. Isn't it encouraging? You're getting so much support from the Catholic priests, and I'm finding a whole new world of help from these Catholic sisters. Is the Lord trying to show us something here?"

For the first time I felt aware of a spiritual union with another person whom I wasn't evangelizing. Here was a coming together of kindred spirits. Suddenly, I felt like the convertee instead of the converter.

When I finished my duties at home in Cartagena, I would hurry to spend free time walking on the beach with these new found "sisters."

We talked for hours. Not having any sisters or brothers of my own, I found a new dimension of friendship and true caring I had never known before. It touched my soul. For the first time in my life, here was a depth of friendship that brought me into peace and happiness as a human being closely connected to others.

Looking back, I have to wonder what effect this bonding had on Glenn. My need for fellowship beyond our marriage was foreign to him.

Earlier I had noticed the carefree way in which Kim had bonded to her little friends in Colombia. Despite the thousands of miles separating their homelands, the cultural barriers, and religious differences, these little playmates were totally one in spirit. They could run and laugh, hold hands, and sing with each other in a pure expression of shared love of life.

Mark also seemed to enjoy being in Colombia. His friends would help him catch fish every day for their four-footed playmates, the cats.

Suddenly the similarity between Kim's and my situation illuminated my heart and mind. I too could walk on the beach, and even hold hands and pray with these Carmelite nuns in a natural friendship. "This is impossible," I caught myself thinking. "How can I enjoy all this time with these friends and feel so totally bonded in the Lord *if* there isn't something to hold us together spiritually?"

Gone were my earlier instincts to proselytize the nuns.

The minute I realized they loved Jesus as much as I did, curiosity about their way of life and personal walk with the Lord engulfed me.

"Marilynn, let me tell you about the works of St. Theresa," one of them offered. Later they introduced me to St. John of the Cross, infused contemplation, and meditation. Here was a total bonding. And it worked in both directions.

Their love for me was equally profound. All of us sensed we would never be the same again.

Every year the Carmelite Missionary Sisters received two weeks of vacation time to visit their families. Several of them gave up all of their annual time to accompany me on my rounds with the Colombian people. Together we taught handicrafts and other arts to the women of San Francisco.

Our working together manifested the truth of the teachings of Vatican II to me personally. The new willingness of the Catholic church to recognize that members of other denominations were Christian was halting bloodshed and hardship for Glenn. It was also binding me together with these believers in a bond that ran deeper than blood. Clearly, these Carmelite nuns across the street from us hadn't simply read the Vatican II documents. They were living them from the heart.

FROM A THREATENED ATTACK WITH MACHETES TO AN ECUMENICAL RALLY

But five hundred years of Colombian reflexes cannot easily change, even when a major church council dictates such change.

One night at San Francisco, Glenn and I were interrupted by a band of men with machetes, who were led by a Catholic priest. "Get out, Senor, and never come back. We don't want your brand of religion."

When a straightforward call for the spirit of Vatican II did nothing to dull the flashing blades, we withdrew for the evening.

"I thought we were beyond these outbursts," lamented Glenn, while making plans to see the archbishop of Cartagena.

"Maybe the Lord has something else big in mind before our tour is over here," I replied.

We had been in Colombia over four years now. General practice for the Assemblies of God church is to recall its missionaries on furlough after five years. Only a matter of months remained on this tour. What else might we hope to accomplish?

Archbishop Isaza of Cartagena was a Franciscan and a beautiful man of God. Upon hearing of the attack, he wrapped his arms around us and said, "Please hang in there. We are one in Jesus. We belong together. God will help us." Then something even more remarkable happened.

"Glenn, I think we should conduct some type of ecumenical rally in the Cartagena stadium," said the archbishop. "That way we can visibly show everyone here that the Catholic church is searching for unity, along with your own group."

So in the final few weeks before making our plans for departure, Glenn and I immersed ourselves in plans for a public rally. I was able to call on my newfound friends from the convent. Glenn had many new supporters throughout the archdiocese.

The rally was a huge success. Approximately five thousand people filled the stadium. Here was a public affirmation of the cooperation between Catholics and missionaries of other denominations. Here was a spontaneous outpouring of love between sheep of kindred flocks. Here was an awakening to new opportunities. And here was the end of our tour in Colombia with the Assemblies of God.

Once we were most prepared to serve, we were forced to leave.

What lay ahead?

FOUR

Pilgrimage of Truth

FIVE YEARS SEEMINGLY DISAPPEARED at the wave of a hand. Now Glenn and I were standing on the top steps of an airplane ramp waving goodbye to our friends in Colombia. But despite the fact the Assemblies of God church required missionaries to take a furlough, I felt confident we would return. Maybe it was the fact that the archbishop of Cartagena pleaded with tears in his eyes, "Please come back to us and help us." Maybe it was because I missed my "sisters" at the Carmelite convent. Maybe it was because Mark felt terrible about leaving his cats with no one to pull fresh fish out of the ocean for them every morning. Or maybe it was because of the large flock of black children from San Francisco, waving so sincerely.

TAKING A RISK: WHERE WOULD IT LEAD?

The Assemblies of God church was eager for us to do promotional work in the United States of America. But Glenn and I were still filled with aspirations for helping the people of Colombia, for interdenominational friendships, and for cooperation with the Catholic church. None of this gave us a firm fix on where we should navigate next for the Lord.

Glenn's brother, John, was a member of a board of an Assemblies of God church in California and the principal of a local high school. He sensed our restlessness.

"Glenn, I have a friend you might be interested in meeting," said John. "He is associated with my high school and happens to be a Catholic priest. Maybe he can help you and Marilynn sort out some of these feelings you've experienced over the past several years and answer some questions." I suspect John felt any person who could handle a campus full of adolescents stumbling through puberty, could probably help us as well.

Fr. James O'Callaghan was pastor of St. John Vianney Church in Hacienda Heights, California. He was the picture of a model Catholic priest: orthodox, Irish, jovial, and always willing to talk—especially if the topic involved faith and its defense!

This handsome defender of the faith took an immediate liking to "any brother of John Kramar." It helped the budding friendship immensely when Fr. O'Callaghan learned of our relationship with the Colombian Catholics and growing hunger for further service.

"Why don't we search and dialogue together," he said, invitingly. "Whatever ray of light comes to us, we'll accept; cost what it may. I hope you're not afraid of where this might lead us!"

"No, Father, I'm not," I answered back in the spirit of the challenge. "We have the full gospel."

"Well, honey, I'm not afraid of it either because I have the whole pie."

There was a great deal of love behind his bravado. Fr. O'Callaghan was not only a defender of the faith, but also a man who loved God, loved the church, and loved all who took an interest in either.

I realized that Glenn and I were taking a risk. But what worthwhile activity doesn't pose a risk? Fr. O'Callaghan gave us a small book entitled *Faith Explained*. We agreed to read one chapter a week and report back for regular discussions.

Along with this intellectual momentum was missionary momentum. Glenn and I continued to visit various churches throughout southern California, promoting Assemblies of God missionary work in Colombia and asking for donations for the building of more churches in Colombia. It was the custom that when missionaries returned from their work overseas, they would visit the churches that had supported them and share their testimonies of missionary life, asking for more support and donations for continued work in their specific countries. They would also encourage the churches to pray for them and take a concern for various missionary projects.

Mark and Kim usually traveled with us. We would all dress up in typical Colombian dress, and Mark would play the guitar. He always had Colombian rhythms running through his veins, and he would sing with me. He was a real charmer, and Kim was a doll. Everyone loved this little missionary girl. I am quite sure we received larger donations merely because of our cute kids.

Every week we would share the outward experience of what had happened in Colombia with fellow members of the Assemblies of God church. At the same time we were sharing the inward experience of our growing respect for the Catholic church with Fr. O'Callaghan.

A GROWING UNDERSTANDING

Both Glenn and I knew we had experienced a real union of the spirit with the nuns and priests of Cartagena. But we were also keenly aware of hundreds of years of theological and doctrinal grievances with the Catholic church. Some of these matched our own personal experiences.

Mary, the Mother of God, required clarification. I had been

brought up to respect this young Jewish girl who was favored by God to bear the Messiah. My own mother expounded the supreme qualities of motherhood modeled by Mary. My dad used her life wonderfully as an example for young Christian women. One day he told me, "Marilynn, if you stay close to Mary you will always be happy." But I never thought of Mary as the "Mother of God" or a "close friend."

First impressions of the Virgin Mary in Latin America were less than impressive. During fiestas and holy days, Mexicans in Guadalajara would dust off their statues of Mary and parade her down the street. Then nearly everybody got drunk or ran out to do battle with another village to see whose virgin was the most popular.

I told Fr. O'Callaghan straight out, "Mary has nothing to do with this. She meant more to me as a human role model than she means to these people who say they are devoted to her."

Patiently, this loyal Catholic explained how he shared my loathing for such abuses. He reminded me that Mary isn't "divine," but rather a "mother" of the church who has a special role to play as an intercessor. He used my examples to highlight the needs that existed within the church for enlightenment, evangelization, and revival. Those were concepts I could appreciate.

"Then explain this one to me, Fr. O'Callaghan," I challenged, moving on to another stumbling block. "I walked into the cathedral in Cartagena and saw a priest standing in front of a long line of people. They wanted him to pray about their problems. But it didn't take me long to notice he wouldn't pray for them unless they slipped some coins into his hand. Here were these dirt-poor people with hardly a stitch of decent clothing being forced to line the silk pockets of a priest before he would present their needs to God. I certainly couldn't live with a situation like that."

"Nor should you," replied Fr. O'Callaghan in his patient

wisdom. "Where can we find people to raise these conditions above such error?"

Another big issue that needed clarification concerned confession. I recognized its importance as a private act between each believer and God. But why must Catholics confess to a priest? And if the repentant soul is freed from the penalty of sin in this manner, why did so many people walk away from the confessional booth with such long faces and forlorn expressions? Where was the love, joy, and peace such penitence brought?

We spent weeks going through this type of questioning with our new friend. At every meeting, we experienced a deeper joy through sharing and a new dimension of spirituality. We discussed baptism in the Holy Spirit and giftedness among the laity. Some of these areas began to spark Fr. O'Callaghan's own curiosity.

THE CHARISMATIC RENEWAL: WERE THERE CATHOLICS WHO WERE PENTECOSTAL AS WELL?

The charismatic renewal movement was only then beginning to get a toehold in the Catholic church. Fr. O'Callaghan, being the mainstream conservative that he was, had avoided most of these innovations. But now here he was sitting face-to-face with a Pentecostal couple in his flock. For despite the fact that Glenn and I were called half a hemisphere away and were not formal members of his church, he was still looking squarely into the eyes of believing laypeople who had already been used by God to spread the gospel. Now we were not the only ones who had to enlarge our understanding of God's new direction in the world.

For mutual enlightenment, Fr. O'Callaghan arranged for us all to meet Fr. Ralph Tichnor, pioneer of the Catholic charismatic renewal at Loyola Marymount University in Los

Angeles. All three of us had questions about this new spirituality. All three were rewarded.

As Fr. O'Callaghan caught a vision of the new possibilities for evangelization and renewal within the church through believers like us, Glenn and I began to fall in love with the Catholic church.

Now I found myself moving beyond the prejudices and beginning to look at the heart of the matter. We had so much in common with the Catholic church at the central core of our beliefs. My understanding of Christ's presence and his visible sign upon us related directly to the seven sacraments in the Catholic faith.

Any lingering doubts about loyalties to the Assemblies of God were laid to rest one evening by a film mix-up in Northern California. We were still seeking missionary funds through these congregations. One evening we were scheduled to speak at a church meeting which had also planned to show a missionary film.

"I'm sorry," said the local pastor. "Our people were expecting to see a film, but the company sent us the wrong one. Do you mind if we show it anyway?"

"What is it?" I asked.

"Something about 'charismatic renewal in the Roman Catholic church,' " he apologized.

"Well it's all right with us if it's all right with you," was my cautious reply. "Maybe we can all learn something."

Before our eyes that evening unfolded the first congress of the renewal at the University of Notre Dame. Bishop Joseph McKinney preached a powerful homily on our need to experience a change of heart. He may not have intended his message for an audience of Pentecostals, but I know that two members of the audience felt a strong need for change in their own hearts—Glenn and I.

For me this movie started bringing everything into focus. Glenn and I both realized there was only one road we could take. There was no turning back. Here in this film was the chalice we had seen in our mutual vision. Here our understanding of the whole gospel was enlarged.

We still wondered how we could embrace a new church as mere laypeople and still fulfill our ambition to serve the brethren in South America. But now our questions switched from "if" to "how."

OUR PROVIDENTIAL MEETING WITH CARDINAL MANNING

Sensing the conflict, Fr. O'Callaghan suggested we meet Cardinal Timothy Manning of the Archdiocese of Los Angeles. His was one of the most widely respected and powerful Catholic leaders in the United States and the world. Naturally we were thrilled by the challenge and only mildly intimidated.

We met for dinner at Fr. O'Callaghan's. Cardinal Manning seemed like a very peaceful Irishman, profoundly enveloped in his love for God. He was a good listener.

The cardinal had just attended a Cursillo movement weekend and felt a great admiration for this experience. The Cursillo experience is designed to bring about a renewed spirit in the church and draw people to a new encounter with Jesus in the life of the sacraments.

Practically the whole dinner conversation that evening focused on how this enlightenment had changed him personally in many ways. Cardinal Manning shared how he previously had found it difficult to exchange a simple handshake, even the Sign of Peace at Mass. To him, personal contact with lay people was not very important. Then, after the first evening on the Cursillo weekend, he discovered how important it is to personally reach out to other human beings and touch them in spirit.

He shared how now he actually yearned to walk down and shake hands at the Sign of Peace with a poor and elderly man who usually sat in the front pew at Mass every morning. Cardinal Manning had hardly noticed this man before. Now he began to give himself away with a new expression of openness. He felt as if he couldn't live through the day without shaking that man's hand at the Sign of Peace. Now he felt comfortable making open expression of his deepest convictions. And that's exactly what the cardinal was doing with us that evening.

It was almost as if this giant of a man in the Catholic church was shedding a cocoon of quietness before our eyes and becoming a grand and glorious butterfly of expression.

What a profound experience for me! I began to feel that my struggle was also a fight to escape some worn-out, unneeded cocoon of the past. Watching this grand leader in the Catholic church expand and cast an even larger shadow before our very eyes made me yearn even more to spread my wings and sail in the warmth of God's new revelation and calling.

Out of that night came the conviction that God not only was calling us to the Catholic church, but giving us a commission as well.

"We don't have a box that you fit into," the cardinal explained. But it was obvious that some type of "box" would be needed to allow a Spirit-filled married couple to carry the mantle of church leadership.

After a great deal of discussion on what we might do, the cardinal offered his blessing in the formation of some type of non-profit society for the purpose of evangelization. Fr. O'Callaghan could serve as the first spiritual director to give it the wisdom and direction available through the Catholic hierarchy. But we would give it wings.

In fact, it was Cardinal Manning who inspired the idea for using a dove in our mission logo with a Providential remark. "Let the bird fly," was how he summed up where and how we should proceed. I have never forgotten that dual invitation and command.

THE PAIN OF LEAVING THE ASSEMBLIES OF GOD

Out of that experience Glenn went back to the Assemblies of God church and turned in our resignation as missionaries. We had no idea of what we would do financially. But we had the living conviction that God was calling us to serve in this new capacity.

Naturally, there was confusion and disappointment among the church leadership in California. We weren't concerned so much about what people might think of us, but we were concerned about what they might think of God.

How would our Colombian brothers and sisters—especially the ones we had evangelized—take this news? Did they share our understanding of the unity of Christ? Would they see our change as an excuse to return to the ungodly ways they had once followed as non-evangelized Catholics? Opportunities would come our way to find out firsthand.

Officially out of the Assemblies of God and not yet officially received into the Catholic church, we were wandering about with no visible means of spiritual support. The only place we could look was toward Fr. O'Callaghan and the St. John Vianney congregation.

Cardinal Manning had already set the gears in motion for the official formation of Charisma in Missions. But the bylaws and articles of incorporation still needed to be hammered out. We expected that.

What we hadn't expected was our need for conditional baptism. After all, if we had been used by Christ with great manifestations of the Spirit to the point that we were recognized by priests and cardinals, how could our baptism be suspect? We learned that the understanding of conditional baptism is very valid in the Catholic church. This means that a person may already have been baptized, but for that to be valid in the Catholic church, a conditional baptism is performed.

We had both been baptized in the Assemblies of God church, but what Fr. O'Callaghan was looking for was a greater clarification. If we were going to be part of the Catholic church, he wanted us to recognize the profound truth of Christ's presence behind the visible signs of the water and the words used in the Rite of Baptism. He wanted us to appreciated the significance that conditional baptism has for Catholic believers. The time required before this conditional baptism could take place would help make sure we deeply understood our own responsibilities and dignity in the Catholic church.

During the process of preparation for conditional baptism, when it looked as though we might need some encouragement, Fr. O'Callaghan said, "Why don't you come and help me start a prayer group in my parish?" I was delighted to say, "Yes."

We had never worked in the charismatic renewal at all and didn't even know how to start such a group, much less to give it direction. We were totally oriented in a different direction. I could get people excited about leaving a parish to minister overseas or to finance missionary work in foreign countries. But I wasn't sure that I could get people excited about bringing a new spirit of dedication to their own parish.

We prayed a lot. That's what made it work from the very first meeting. Fr. O'Callaghan called his whole parish together for an orientation on what it meant to pray together and search for the gifts of the Spirit. Glenn and I probably learned more than the rest of the congregation at that first meeting.

We didn't see ourselves as outsiders coming in, or as spiritually superior people handing down teaching from on high. Rather, we were so excited about the gifts of the Holy Spirit and felt such a love and spiritual oneness with the people of the parish—it was only natural to share the charismatic dimension of our spirituality with them.

Soon we had approximately three hundred people coming to those prayer meetings every week. These were

English speaking, middle-to-upper income people from all over the San Gabriel Valley.

Things were happening quickly during this short span of time from December, 1972 to May, 1973. And while we were both teaching and studying the Catholic faith, I felt a compelling urge to return to Colombia to discern firsthand what God would do through us in our newfound love of the Catholic faith and desire for ministry.

While the response of many at the Assemblies of God to our decision to become Catholic had been disappointing, my dad's response was beautiful. I kept wondering what this devoted Pentecostal minister thought of his turncoat daughter. Soon he made it abundantly clear. Mom and Dad had accompanied Glenn and me to the airport to see us off to Colombia.

"Mom and Dad, I have something to tell you before I leave the country. Maybe you had better sit down for this news," I announced as they looked at me in surprised anticipation. "I think when we get back from this trip we are going to become Catholics."

Then it was Dad's turn to surprise me. "Well, honey," he said. "I think you had better be the one to sit down. I want to tell you that we've always believed you were in the perfect will of God. We will never lose any sleep over you and will always back you. We will always be with you."

I gave them both a big hug. And though I was boarding the plane for a trip of thousands of miles, I never felt closer to my parents or to my Creator.

OUR RETURN TO LATIN AMERICA

Even during takeoff from Los Angeles International Airport, I remember looking down and thinking, "We'll never be the same." I felt overwhelmed with conviction, almost breathless and faint in my awareness of this new role in life. Glenn shared this passion with me. We were enjoying the winds of change and were unified in our purpose.

Upon arrival in Colombia we decided upon a risky course of action. We would immediately approach the archbishop of Medellin.

Located in the interior of Colombia, Medellin is the most conservative Catholic city in the nation—perhaps in the Latin world. At that time it didn't carry the stigma it now bears as the drug-producing capital of the world. Glenn went directly to Archbishop Tulio Botero and shared what was happening to us. We offered ourselves to do whatever he might need. This excited the archbishop.

"I want you to meet our bishop who lives in Sonson-Rionegro. He is from the same archdiocese and has become curious over what is happening in this movement of the Spirit. I think you should go and talk to him."

Archbishop Botero sent a Jesuit priest, Florencio Alvarez, to accompany us on our trip to Sonson-Rionegro. Fr. Alvarez was a one-man pep squad for Scripture and evangelistic renewal. Though small and elderly, this energetic disciple drove a small jeep and was known in every convent and seminary in the region. He was so active in the promotion of the Scripture and renewal that he seemed to know everybody and everything.

Fr. Alvarez not only took us to Bishop Alfonso Aribe Jaramillo in Sonson-Rionegro, but he immediately transported us from convent to convent, from seminary to seminary, school to school. He was thrilled to help us share what was happening in our lives through the Lord's revelation to us of the Catholic faith and the charismatic renewal, especially as we had understood it from the documents of Vatican II.

Bishop Jaramillo invited us to give a retreat to his priests and nuns. He warned them not to pay too much attention to our outward expressions, because "we don't do things like touch, feel, applaud, or such." He admonished them, "Pay attention to what the Kramars are trying to say in regards to the work of the Spirit."

One incident occurred which made me grateful for Bishop Jaramillo's patience and understanding.

This happened at one of the retreats we were giving for Franciscan nuns within the city of Medellin. The topic was our basic material on "Life in the Spirit." In presenting the segment on "The Work of the Holy Spirit and the Charismatic Gifts of the Spirit," my approach was still based on what I learned and practiced in the Assemblies of God. We placed heavy emphasis on speaking in tongues. I didn't know any better. We were still learning how all this teaching on spiritual gifts relates to different people from various backgrounds and formations.

So without even thinking, I reached back into my experience in the Assemblies of God to illustrate the point. People in our former church were deeply concerned about the time at which someone would finally speak in tongues as proof that they had received the Holy Spirit. The promotion of speaking in tongues was still a big part of our presentation.

We finished our segment with little evidence on the part of these nuns that anything was happening through the Spirit. At the end of the day, we were all sitting in a circle, and one nun blurted out something in another tongue. Then she gave the interpretation in Spanish. Naturally, I became extremely happy and overjoyed. This "proved" they must have learned and responded.

When the entire retreat was finished and I was walking out of the convent, the mother superior turned to me and said, "Now are you happy?"

We had become pretty close friends by this time. But I still had to ask, "What do you mean?"

"Are you happy you finally got to hear one of the nuns speaking in tongues and giving the interpretation?"

"Yes."

"I'm sorry to have to tell you this, Marilynn," she continued, "but you missed the whole beauty of this entire weekend. You have walked through this experience without ever becoming aware of the beauty of God's presence in what he was doing in the life of our sisters. You were only interested in getting them to speak in tongues."

That criticism struck me to the core from her first sentence. But she continued to explain what God had done through us, through the whole retreat in bringing to her sisters a new awareness of their first love, and how my focus on exterior actions and emotions had almost trampled these delicate blossoms. I had much to learn about deeper manifestations of sincere renewal.

Naturally, the truth hurt. But fortunately wounds administered in love come with their own healing balm. From that day on I laid myself at the feet of the bishops and tried to understand more fully how my own experiences related to the experiences God has already invested in other Spirit-filled servants.

From these encounters, Bishop Jaramillo started over two hundred fifty prayer groups within a matter of only six months in his small diocese made up primarily of coffee growers. He was courageous enough to start a prayer group in his own house. There he would invite the coffee growers to come and sit on the floor with him for prayer. Among the bishops in the Latin world, he is one of those best known for encouraging renewal among Catholics. He has founded seminaries that are now packed with students preparing for missionary work throughout Latin America.

His hunger for the Word of God was a tremendous example and motivation to us. Though he continually thanked us for bringing our message into his country and teaching his people, we felt grateful for all he had taught us. I consider it a tremendous opportunity to have sat at the feet of Bishop Alfonso Jaramillo of Medellin. He gave us a greater understanding of how the renewal we were experiencing was related to Jesus Christ who is the "heart of the church" and the visible signs of his presence through the sacraments.

NO LONGER SPIRITUAL VAGRANTS

This trip lasted about six weeks. Upon our return, Glenn and I were more determined than ever to follow through with conditional baptism into the Catholic church.

It occurred in May 1973, and all of our family attended. This included the Robertses, the Kramars, and our intimate friends and brothers from St. John Vianney Church. They were all there to welcome Glenn, Mark, Kim, and me into the Catholic church through conditional baptism.

Fr. O'Callaghan told me about a beautiful tradition that accompanies baptism—one that became even more beautiful for me since I had already fulfilled it in advance. Upon baptism a believer often receives a new Christian name. But for me that wasn't necessary. My name, Marilynn, can be traced back to a dynamic believer recognized by the Catholic church. Fr. O'Callaghan told me that "Mari" was the name of a second-century woman evangelist. I could use that as my Christian name for baptism.

Cardinal Manning even sent us a gift for the occasion. We didn't understand its full significance at the time, but we have grown to appreciate it more and more as the years go by. It was an attractive medallion of "Our Lady of the Angels," the statue of Mary that stands in the cathedral of Los Angeles. What we didn't realize was that the name "Los Angeles" is associated with St. Francis of Assisi. A chapel in Assisi called *Porciuncula* or "small portion" is said to be the one used by St. Francis for personal devotion after he became committed to the work of austerity and spiritual renewal. Tradition says that when he went there to pray, the sound of angels could be heard coming out of the chapel walls. This "small portion" with the angelic voices was later donated to St. Francis as his first missionary quarters and center for his work of evangelization.

Years later, when the Franciscans came to Southern California to found their missionary work, they named their city "The Village of Our Lady the Queen of the Angels of Porciuncula" now shortened to "Los Angeles."

Two years after receiving this baptismal gift, Glenn and I had occasion to travel to Italy. We were attending the first world conference on the charismatic renewal in the Catholic church. We took the opportunity to visit Assisi and tour that same chapel.

Then the realization struck me. I was coming back full circle to the point at which the Catholic church started one of its own great renewals to study renewal so I could spread renewal. This "small portion" at Porciuncula made a large impact on me—so large in fact that it affected the name of our CharisMissions Center.

"Marilynn, I think Cardinal Manning would like to name the center," our spiritual director told me a few years later when we had grown to the point of having our own buildings. "Why don't you give him that liberty?"

I gladly asked the cardinal to do the honors for us. Before he actually came to the dedication of the center, he called me in one day and said, "Marilynn, I want to ask you before I actually name this center if you had any inclinations about what you might want the center to be called. I'd like to see if I am in line with what you feel."

I thought a moment and replied, "Well, the only inclination I have is that it should represent something of Franciscan spirituality. You see, Cardinal Manning, ever since our first experience with the people of San Francisco in Cartagena, Colombia, the gift you gave us at baptism, and the whole concept of the spirit of poverty, I would want it to say something about the life of St. Francis. And it should be strongly Marian, because I love Mary."

Pilgrimage of Truth / 99

"You've got it," he replied with enthusiasm. "It's the 'Porciuncula,' the 'small portion' of St. Francis."

It would appear the cardinal had actually named our center long before it was conceived through a well chosen gift at our conditional baptism.

Today that same gift with its inscription to "Our Lady of the Angels of Porciuncula" is displayed on the altar in our chapel. It rests on a rock from the actual chapel of Porciuncula. A Franciscan priest collected one of the stones with permission and gave it to us when we were there on a later visit. Ever since our baptism (and even before), we have never been far from the foundations of St. Francis in our spirituality.

OUR MINISTRY IN THE CHURCH

But that's getting ahead of our story.

Soon after my baptism, Fr. O'Callaghan asked if I would teach a Bible study class for women of the parish. Then he required that his catechism teachers attend the class.

As the charismatic prayer meeting we led and this class as well grew in numbers, we felt more and more comfortable in our new roles of ministry among Catholics. Other leaders from throughout the parish attended regularly to imbibe of the charismatic spirit (and respond to Fr. O'Callaghan's orders). I felt very much at home.

That made the next step seem totally natural. As we shared our love for the church, which emanated straight from the heart, we couldn't help sharing our heart's desires as well. With these various groups of executives, women, teachers, and parish leaders our prayers begin to turn once again to the destitute people of Colombia.

Here was the core of another loyal missionary support group. Fr. O'Callaghan even allowed us to collect some offerings.

As in the streets of Colombia, once again everything we touched began turning to gold. With Fr. O'Callaghan's guidance, we even started giving retreats and missions outside the parish and throughout the archdiocese.

We would use the Scriptures and the documents of Vatican II in our presentations and proclamations in various parishes and missions. The Scriptures and this council provided a deep sense of identity for us as lay leaders. They outlined our mission in the church—to rattle new life into dry bones within the household of God. The first Christians went out to evangelize and to baptize new converts. Our job was to evangelize baptized Catholics who either didn't fully understand or were not actively involved in the life of faith.

MANIFESTATIONS OF THE SPIRIT IN BOGOTA

About this time, Glenn and I had occasion to go back to Bogota for a short while. I wanted to visit our old friend Fr. Garcia Herreros. During the years of our pilgrimage from the Assemblies of God to the Catholic church, we made at least eight or nine trips of varying lengths back to Colombia. They were extremely helpful to me in defining the scope and direction of our new spiritual journey. The following instance proved to be one of the high points.

There at Bogota I was invited to visit a Benedictine girls' school in one of the high class parts of town. Glenn wasn't with me at the time, and I wanted to make a good accounting of myself as a servant of the Spirit.

The local nuns were interested in the charismatic renewal, but didn't really know how to proceed. They asked me to help them present a retreat for the local schoolgirls.

We decided to present short messages on the love of God and the consequences of sin. I finished my talk on God's love and concluded with prayer. All of a sudden several of these girls began to experience strong manifestations of the

Spirit. I didn't do anything to bring this on. I was sure. We weren't even discussing manifestations of the spirit.

All of a sudden something struck them with an overwhelming impact. Some began crying. Others were praying in the Spirit. One girl stood up and began speaking in tongues. Phenomenal things were happening all around us.

The girl with the gift of tongues started writing phrases on the blackboard in a language she didn't even know. One of the nuns, who was German, looked up at the board and began translating everything the girl was writing.

Other nuns came running in. The teachers wanted to know what was happening. I was at a loss to explain.

What happened next was a complete surprise. I had never experienced anything like this before. Somehow I became smitten with a holy gift of laughter. I was embarrassed and wanted to stop, but I doubled over laughing. When the bell rang for class to end and the girls began lining up to board the buses, I was still standing in the corner immersed in laughter.

Jeannette, the young girl with the gift of tongues, left the room speaking in another language. She boarded the bus with her girl friends and kept on praying in the Spirit in another language.

The nuns led me off to the office, laughter filling the hallways. They didn't know what to do with me, with themselves, or with the girls.

A few minutes later we got a call from Jeannette's parents. "What did you do to my girl? Why doesn't she speak Spanish? She won't even speak English. That we could understand."

"Bring her back to school in the morning," said one of the nuns for lack of anything better to suggest. "We'll explain what happened and get everything straightened out."

Next morning I walked into a room full of teachers, psychologists, reporters, and Jeannette's perplexed parents. Her father was a well-known doctor in the city who had had a heart attack and was recuperating at home. His wife was a nervous wreck.

Jeannette handed me a note in English. "Don't worry about me. I'm just with Jesus." I grabbed and shook her and said, "Jeannette, for God's sake speak in Spanish." No results. She retired to a corner and sat there lost in her own world.

Then I was faced with the task of explaining this whole episode to all the curious onlookers. They begin writing and taking notes furiously.

At the end of this meeting, when the questions were over and everyone felt they knew what was going on, up walked one of the nuns who had had nothing to do with the previous events. She became red in the face and started trembling. As all eyes focused on her unusual behavior, she opened her mouth and started prophesying in the midst of all these people. Once again the pencils flew.

After the meeting Jeannette went home and continued speaking in tongues for a full seven days.

Things quieted down enough for me to return to Los Angeles. Then it was up to Fr. Garcia Herreros to explain everything. I was afraid the incident would bring discredit in the church. But I wasn't giving enough credit to Fr. Herreros.

His explanation went to the whole country via newspaper and television, describing the work of God's mighty Spirit at the Benedictine girls' school. He presented it as a manifestation of a powerful renewal sweeping through the Catholic church in Colombia. He was spectacular. He wrote articles on the event and the newspapers ran the whole story. I still have some of those articles today.

Glenn and I returned soon after that and met with Fr. Herreros on TV. We announced our first youth congress in Colombia in conjunction with him. Thousands of young people came to that congress through the television invitations.

Out of this experience I learned that Marilynn Kramar had a great deal more to offer the world than music and wifely advice. God had a special call on my life that was just now starting to come into focus. Reflecting on all that had taken place as we returned to minister in Colombia, I also realized that life would probably never be the same in regard to former relationships with the Assemblies of God missionaries in Colombia.

Word spread fast about Glenn and Marilynn Kramar. Most of our acquaintances were in a quandary about how to relate to our conditional baptism in the Catholic church. Some thought we had sold out to the "Whore of Babylon." Most simply didn't know how to react.

They had known our zeal for Christ and our dedication to the Colombian people. Fear overtook some of them as they thought of future Assemblies of God missionaries who might come to minister in Colombia and who would want to follow in our footsteps. The Colombian members of the Assemblies of God as a whole remained sorrowful. They wanted us to return to them. It was difficult for us as well. Even with our new-found joys, we couldn't adequately defend or put into words how we felt. We didn't know how to explain that, although we had converted to the Catholic faith, Jesus Christ was the shepherd of both traditions.

NEW DIMENSIONS IN THE SPIRIT

Upon return to Los Angeles after the initial incident with the manifestations of the Spirit at the girls' school, I was so high with enthusiasm for the Lord, I rushed to share it with one of his fellow servants: Fr. O'Callaghan.

Naturally, I called him over to hear the whole story. When he came to the front door, I practically leapt into his arms and grabbed him and hugged him. I was so excited and overjoyed and thankful in my heart for what God had given me through this man. He helped me share my life with so many people! I know that through him God had blessed me with the gift of a whole new life. All of these feelings flowed out through my emotional greeting. No telling what this customarily reserved man was thinking at the time. But I wanted him to know how much good all of his patient effort with Glenn and me had accomplished for so many other people.

I don't know if it was that single heartfelt greeting, or if it was the culmination of so much work on our behalf, or if there were other forces shaping the life of Fr. O'Callaghan. But he changed. From that day forward, this sometimes cold and distant cleric, certainly unaccustomed to physical contact, much less hugging, turned into a warm, expressive brother. Now he continually opens himself up to others and lets them hug him, too. To this very day, he still hugs me every time we meet. He has learned not only to give affection to his congregation, but to receive it as well.

I saw the same lesson learned over and over again in the lives of most everyone I met throughout this pilgrimage from the Assemblies of God to the Catholic church, myself included. Where people were once concerned about "God and me alone," now they are opening up to the needs and emotions of their fellow human beings. It was almost as if God had looked down and said, "If you want a special relationship with me, do something special for those I love."

Today Fr. O'Callaghan is a monsignor and, among parish priests, one of those most actively involved in renewal. I have never seen a parish more renewed than his. It promotes the active role of the laity in parish life. It has grown tremendously. Today there are over ten thousand parishioners. It's an amazing place. I like to think I had a small part in helping encourage the monsignor's growth in personal expressiveness.

OUT OF THE CLOUDS

Shortly after my return from Bogota, Fr. O'Callaghan introduced me to Bishop Juan Arzube, vicar for the Spanish-speaking people in the Archdiocese of Los Angeles. Both men felt that my contagious enthusiasm would be a good innoculation against apathy and complacency in things of the Spirit among the local Hispanic community. It seems it was the heyday of political activism and not spiritual renewal among Hispanics in California.

"But first I want to take you out of the clouds and bring you down into the reality of what is happening in California. Then maybe you can help us accomplish something for the Hispanic people in the archdiocese," said Bishop Arzube.

A retreat was scheduled at the seminary in Camarillo, California. This beautiful community is about sixty miles northwest of Los Angeles, not too far inland from where the sun and the sky meet the California coast. What I learned there certainly dropped me from the clouds.

The meeting hall was filled with Hispanic priests, nuns, and lay leaders from all over the state. Cesar Chavez, along with the farm hands of California, were deeply involved in the changes necessary to initiate a union for the rights of the Spanish-speaking farm workers. Together with these leaders from the church, he was searching for ways of making these changes.

I'll never forget walking in and feeling the animosity. People were shouting into the microphone, *"Que viva la huelga*—Long live the strike." Others were trying to hammer their opinions of justice and social concern into anyone who would listen. Here was a whole new world for me.

Bishop Arzube had asked me to help begin some type of spiritual renewal and evangelization among Hispanics in the Los Angeles area. It was inspiring to see that out of such antagonism and confrontation a spirit of love and cooperation could dawn.

Now I was in the Catholic church, heart and soul, and face-to-face with current issues in Southern California. My pilgrimage to another altar was complete, and there were obviously many people to serve.

Had I fully counted the cost? This answer proved to be important because bills from many unexpected quarters came rolling in.

FIVE

The Price of Obedience

ONE OF OUR FIRST SACRIFICES was financial. We simply didn't have a reliable income. Father O'Callaghan allowed us to collect money from the parish prayer group for missionary work in Colombia, and that was about it. Thank God I knew what it meant to sell fly swatters.

Our home office was in my father's old studio in Fullerton. His former secretary helped us record tapes for use in Colombia. We produced a series on "The Seven Steps to Abundant Life." This included "Introduction to the life of the Spirit," "Love of God," "Conversion," "Life in the Holy Spirit" (including the charismatic gifts), and "The Continual Life of Prayer."

The St. John Vianney prayer group financed forty-two tapes in Spanish during our first year. They became so excited about themselves as laity being able to support missionary work in Latin America. The joy of our conversion seemed to carry them forward in promoting work that was instrumental in our renewal efforts.

It was exciting to see the tapes in use. We sent copies or presented them personally to leaders like Fr. Garcia Herreros and others who were desiring the promotion of evangelization and renewal. Tapes worked their way to convents and seminary schools.

We never knew where they would turn up next. The distribution system was fabulous. One convent could distribute material to every community and every school in its region. On later trips to Colombia, I often heard our recorded messages and music playing on main plazas to whole communities. This was in the early 1970's, when the tape cassette recorder was coming into its own. It showed us the Lord's perfect timing.

The tapes were welcome and effective, but not very lucrative for us as a means of paying our own bills. We tried to supplement our income with a newsletter.

It was called "CharisMissions"; its a logo showed Jesus holding a Bible in his hand and an hourglass. It promoted renewal, but unfortunately it didn't do much for helping us make ends meet.

Raising money proved much harder in Catholic congregations than in Protestant ones. Many were unaccustomed to the idea of evangelization through lay members—much less raising money to pay for it.

We may have been struggling financially, but we still felt the joy of our first love for the Catholic church. For us this was greater security than a mere paycheck.

We felt the Lord was calling us to make a commitment to live what they call in the Catholic church "a vow of poverty." One hundred percent of our life seemed to be enveloped in this mission. We only expected that God would provide enough to pay our rent and our basic necessities. If this was of God, we felt certain he would show us ways to accomplish it financially.

We tried not to let our financial concerns burden Mark and Kim. We lived from day to day only by the discovery that we had enough food to eat and enough clothes to cover our children and enough money to pay our rent. Many times I harkened back to my own "fly swatter" days. But we were together as a family, and I suppose that, in itself, made life more bearable.

We never wanted to become wealthy. In our hearts, we identified with the needs of the people. And their level of subsistence was far from luxurious.

I am indeed grateful for the way God has multiplied the ministry of CharisMissions. There is a growing need for new instruments of service within the church. Every year more religious orders and convents are closing their doors because they say that there are no more vocations. But we have observed there is a world of vocations to be lived; it's just that most of them don't fall within the prescribed definitions of the past.

Maybe the Lord is raising up organizations such as CharisMissions among the laity to perform missionary work around the world. They have to be supported somehow, and I feel blessed that we have been able to serve as pioneers.

THE BIRTH OF THE *ENCUENTRO LATINO*

Along with Bishop Juan Arzube, we envisioned an *Encuentro Latino* for renewal and reconciliation of the Hispanic community. We contacted all the leaders in the area and invited everyone we could from throughout the archdiocese and other areas of California. The first *Encuentro Latino* took place in 1975 in the San Gabriel Mission outside of Los Angeles. Approximately six hundred attended. They came from Los Angeles and throughout California, as well as from Mexico and other Latin American countries.

We encouraged the priests who had become involved in the charismatic renewal in Latin America, and those we had met during our travels, to join us. Our focus was to proclaim the good news to the Hispanic people in order to evangelize alienated Catholics, as well as to give teachings for those who desired to become more involved in the work of evangelization and renewal.

The Spirit of the Lord was on this event in a remarkable

way. People caught the vision and became very much associated with CharisMissions. It was more than teaching or catechetical instruction. It was a direct calling for reconciliation and renewal in the personal lives of the participants.

While the tape ministry also continued to spread throughout the Latin world, the desire for monthly evangelization and renewal through assemblies and rallies also grew. Thus, they became a regular part of our ministry.

We began to conduct rallies here in Los Angeles similar to the Billy Graham Evangelistic Campaign approach. I remember watching him once on television. People by the thousands streamed down to profess Jesus as Lord.

I thought, "My God, this message should be developed for a Catholic audience. We need to act upon our faith response and be reconciled and renewed. We need to live an authentic life of faith in the Lord." The seal of all these manifestations of the Spirit and responses in faith is the celebration of the Eucharist for a Catholic. In my mind's eye it was clear what such a rally could mean to our Hispanic people and how it might be organized. As Catholic evangelists, we would proclaim the good news using lively music and testimony. We would call for a reconciliation with Christ and then celebrate the Mass in order to seal this commitment in the Body and Blood of Jesus Christ.

Naturally, we were excited about the opportunity to proclaim the Good News and to celebrate the visible sign of Christ's presence and power to heal and forgive through the Eucharist.

It became clear how God was leading. There was a sincere desire to affirm and grow in the work of renewal and evangelization. It allowed us to affirm and evangelize ourselves as Catholics to the heart of the church. From the rallies and assemblies, there also grew a need for follow-up ministries.

One of the first ministries we provided was an initial

evangelization course to reach the baptized. This was to evangelize them through a personal renewal of the sacraments of baptism, confirmation, and the Eucharist.

A BALANCED AND SOLID THEOLOGY FOR MINISTRY

On paper, it may not sound like the most exciting development, but we learned the basics of Catholic theology from a Holy Spirit Missionary Father in Mexico. What he taught us was foundational for our ministry. From him we learned the main steps in evangelizing the laity at the heart of the church. The process involves renewing the sacraments of initiation in the lives of baptized Catholics, so they become concrete realities and effective channels of grace.

In baptism, first there is a calling to new life in Jesus, then a realization that the old man has passed away. As the new man comes forth, he is transformed into an "ambassador for Christ" and participates in the ministry of Christ to the entire body. In confirmation, we receive not only the gifts of the Spirit as we would know them in the charismatic renewal, but our basic call to live for Jesus by imitating his virtues.

We see the fruits of the Spirit being cultivated in our lives, while the power of baptism in the Holy Spirit awakens us to the ongoing potential for new life—the ever-flowing stream of living water bubbling up to eternal life. From that union in the Spirit, the Eucharist calls us to a relationship with Jesus and each other in a community of love where we can again say, "We are church."

Glenn and I tried to capture the essence of this theology in our courses. We began to promote this new understanding not only among the attendees of the *Encuentro Latino,* but within the parishes of the Los Angeles area. We also helped people who were being called to these ministries learn how to become evangelizers themselves. This initiation course for evangelization ministries has now reached thousands of Latinos in California, all over the United States, and in many other Latin American countries.

Through the hardships and doubts, Glenn and I took heart from examples such as Andres and Rosario Lopez.

For twenty-five years Andres was an alcoholic, drinking more than a gallon of whiskey every two days. He abused his wife and children and trapped the entire family in a downward spiral headed for divorce and destruction. He wanted to change, but he couldn't do it on his own before coming to our rallies.

At one point, Andres became so despondent and guilt-ridden that he planned to end his life on the freeway by steering his car into a telephone pole. At the exact moment he decided to commit suicide, the Lord (whom he didn't even recognize at this point in his life) said, "Andres, stop! I love you." God intervened directly in his life to awaken him to who he really was and what a blessing his family was to him! His full and vibrant return to the Christian life then came through an *Encuento Latino*.

I am humbled to think our rallies and initiation courses were a tool in this transformation. Not only did Andres become a stable and loving presence to his family, he also caught the vision of what it means to live sacramentally in his own marriage and family life.

Soon he and his wife began to multiply their personal healing in the lives of hundreds of other couples by getting involved in the work of personal renewal and evangelization. Andres and his wife had met Christ at the heart of the church, had brought that reality into their own home, and were now eagerly sharing the good news with others.

Even though the Lord was working in such powerful ways through our ministry, the costs to us personally were taking their toll—not necessarily in financial strain. That we could see in black and white. These costs were measured in terms of human anguish.

COUNTING THE COST

Jesus tells us in one of his parables that no one can build a tower without "counting the cost." Otherwise, he may only finish half of it and run out of resources. I'm sorry to report that is essentially what was happening to us.

Pastor Robert Schuller says that life is a time of "nesting, testing, and cresting." We had built our nest and were about to face an enormous test. Only now as I write, some fifteen years later after overcoming some devastating falls, can I say we are cresting the challenge.

It all started when several bishops in Colombia encouraged Glenn to attend a seminary in Rome. One of them was specifically designed for late vocations to the priesthood. The bishops would help ask for an exception at the Vatican for Glenn's status as a married priest for Latin America.

I am sure that if we could have sat down at that point together and literally counted the cost as two human beings in one spirit as husband and wife, we may not have jumped into this as quickly as we did. But it's hard to put the blame on anything other than zeal, enthusiasm, and love for the church. Maybe there were other unspoken motivations for recognition and the excitement of leadership that were acting on us as well.

We had traveled to Rome together in 1975 for the international Catholic charismatic congress. At that time the doors opened for Glenn to study at the Beta College for late vocations. We were both excited about the possibilities for ministry, but saddened and concerned about the separation it required.

With our new and vibrant monthly rallies, the weight of CharisMissions was mounting. Up to this point, I had totally depended upon Glenn for our administrative decisions. I was a good executive secretary and worked along with him, but I was never in direct office management. This would put a strain on both of us. The strain extended to our children as well.

Sometimes we expect too much of our children. We share our hopes and ambitions with them as adults in ministry. But still they can only perceive on a childlike, human level. At the age of fourteen, Mark bravely declared, "Dad, I'll do anything you want me to do. I'll do anything for your priesthood." Easy to profess, this proved more than he could deliver.

Kim, age eleven, was Daddy's little princess, his adorable doll. She had a strong temperament and reassured us, "We'll make it somehow, you know." Kim was partially right.

Leaving Glenn in Rome, I returned to a burgeoning ministry. I started the first of three monthly rallies with about two hundred fifty people. Soon we would outgrow the San Gabriel auditorium and move into the Shrine auditorium in downtown Los Angeles.

The workload was mounting.

The children and I flew out to visit Glenn after a few months in December of 1976. We stayed several days with him at the seminary and decided to take a vacation together.

This should have been a joyous reunion. But I began to feel that our lives were separating. Glenn was moving toward another way of life and thought altogether. Naturally, a great deal of things had happened to me in Los Angeles as I had grown into my new responsibilities as the leader of CharisMissions. Perhaps this made Glenn uncomfortable. Perhaps he was unsure of his own abilities and identity. Perhaps he was getting exposed to new ideas and new priorities.

I was hearing things that bothered me enormously. Glenn was starting to make light of newcomers in the seminary who "were making total fools out of themselves by coming down the halls at night praising God and shouting 'hallelujah' in the hallways." He was referring to the external expressions of the charismatic renewal movement that had meant so much to us and that point to so much more than mere externals. He talked about new moral theology and his future intentions for a life in the ministry.

One day Glenn took Mark to his room and showed him a collection of liquor bottles and the new pipe he was now smoking.

All of this amounted to an almost total rejection of our past. It was as if he had shut the door to any type of charismatic influence in his new train of thought. I felt that could only mean he was shutting the door on me as well.

Doubts and struggles from his past welled up to influence his goals for the future. I heard him brooding over boyhood experiences in church and other areas of his life. I didn't know him any more in the Spirit. It seemed as though we had nothing in common. Even the friendships I had developed for companionship during his absence seemed to provoke him to jealousy.

When he returned for the summer of 1977, he tried to get involved in our mission work again, but nothing made sense to him. Where once we had agreed on fundamental doctrines such as sin and its consequences, now he wasn't sure sin even existed.

No one really knew him. We had experienced so much growth that many of our new followers knew nothing about "Marilynn's husband in Rome." And those who did remember him were perplexed at his lack of enthusiasm for what was happening in their lives.

He attended some of our rallies, but it seemed that he was in total turmoil. All he could bring himself to do was sit and watch. His heart was not in it anymore.

A GODSEND: ESTHER RETURNS

During this time, the workload of the new mission and monthly rallies became increasingly burdensome on me and my small office staff with no real administrative help. I desperately needed assistance. "Lord, you know I can't do this on my own. Please send someone I can rely on to help."

God answered this prayer in a most heartwarming way. During one of our recent trips to Colombia, I rediscovered Esther Garzon. This was the same young girl who had helped us so much in Bogota when Glenn was first thrust into the office of national superintendent for the Assemblies of God church. Unknown to us, she, too, had converted to the Catholic faith. Glenn and I had asked her to help us in the work of coordination for CharisMissions in Colombia. Now she was with me once again on an extended visit.

Finding her the first time as a fellow Assemblies of God member in Colombia was a joy. Learning she had converted to Catholicism was miraculous. Having her join me here in California was a godsend. Now I wondered if she would extend the miracle and consent to stay here and help me through these tumultuous times. Kim loved her and I needed her not as a secretary, but as a friend. This bashful little girl had grown into a strong proclaimer of the faith.

One evening as Esther was sitting on the couch with me watching TV, I approached her with my heartfelt request. I knew how much she disliked the idea of remaining in the United States and of her desire to return to Colombia. I reviewed my feelings to make sure I was responding to the will of the Lord and not my own desires. "Esther, I think God wants you to stay here with me."

"Marilynn, I don't have to think about it much at all. Last night, the Lord told me I should stay here," she answered.

Fortunately, the bureaucratic red tape of getting her green card for residency went smoothly. Little did I know at that point how much I really needed her support and comfort.

When Glenn returned to Rome for his second year of studies for the priesthood, I found myself questioning our relationship and future ministry. There was nothing tangible I could point to, beyond my feelings and impressions during recent visits with him. Unfortunately, when someone is far away, all you have to hold on to is your feelings and impressions of that person. When those are injured, the entire relationship can be jeopardized.

After his second year, Glenn was ready for the diaconate toward his priesthood. Yet word came down from Rome that he was "not accepted for the priesthood at this time." It wasn't necessarily a permanent rejection, but he seemed to take it that way.

He returned to California a broken and confused man. His hopes for the priesthood and prestige were gone. As he saw his wife on the rise and his own "career" as such on the rocks, he fell into turmoil. All that remained was his disgust for charismatics and an immense identity crisis.

GLENN FINDS ANOTHER LOVE

Driven from the arms of the life he had sought and the wife he had lived with for twenty years, Glenn rebounded into the arms of a woman he desired.

Glenn had met her in California before he ever traveled to Rome. She was a former Franciscan nun who had entered the convent when she was thirteen. Upon leaving the convent, she found herself searching for new friends and a sense of community. When we first met her, she was struggling to rebuild her life. We felt led to befriend her.

While Glenn was back in Rome, she came to work for CharisMissions. Once he returned, their romance was obvious. It seemed that they were in great confusion.

"Friends, we are only as brother St. Francis and sister St. Clare," he announced to the stunned office workers one day. The two of them felt they had "the right" to commune with the trees, roam through the parks, and pick flowers.

I was devastated by what was going on.

One weekend I asked if he wanted to go with me to one of our missionary meetings in Lancaster, California.

"No thanks, I'll just stay here," he said.

118 / The Marilynn Kramar Story

Esther and I went to the meeting and had to spend the night there. I called back to see how he was doing. Glenn wasn't home. When I called the Community House, they told me, "No, he's out looking for an apartment for her."

When I finally got him on the phone at midnight, I asked him outright, "Are you having an affair with her?"

"Yes."

He went on to explain that he couldn't live a lie any longer. He loved her. And he wanted me to give him permission to have this friendship with her. He didn't say a word about wanting to separate from me. He simply wanted to have her as well.

I was shattered and felt my life had come to an end. Esther watched me bang my fist on the floor and shout at Glenn, at God, and at the whole situation.

This period of confusion lasted for about six months. Nothing made sense anymore. We were all suffering.

Glenn was living with me, but dwelling with her. Our office staff watched them come and go as some sort of irresponsible free spirits. One night he replaced his shoes with sandals and declared again that he was simple like St. Francis. One minute he was an executive, the next minute Glenn didn't even want to dress in a business suit for speaking engagements.

His frequent uncomplimentary remarks were like a verbal knife going through me. He would call me, "Kathryn Kuhlman," making fun of a woman God had so mightly used in ministry and showing again his total misunderstanding of what was happening in my life.

Everything came to a head on December 31, 1977. I was planning a New Year's Mass at our home, but the family tension was unbearable. Our community came together in prayer, and we cried out, "Lord, you know what we are suffering. Please solve this problem for us. We give you permission to do whatever you have to do in order to set things right. And please, Lord, what you have to do, do quickly. We can't live in this confusion and anguish any longer."

Later that evening Glenn came to the Mass. He told the community he was leaving his marriage, the community, and everything. I can't say it was a surprise, but the sadness and shock of this trauma seemed more than I could bear.

About two weeks later on a Sunday morning (I still remember the exact date), January 17, 1978, Glenn walked in to say a final goodbye to the children.

"Daddy is going to leave," he told the children. To Mark, he said, "You're now responsible for the household. You'll have to take responsibility for your mom and your sister. I must go."

Through the tears, Kim stood at the door and called out, "Why are you leaving us? Why do you have to go?"

What can a girl of thirteen understand about broken promises and infidelity? I picked her up off the floor and took her to my mother's place.

It was the day of the monthly rally, *Presencia*. And I didn't know how I could possibly make it through the afternoon at a public event. Details are a blur in my mind. But somehow I got prepared and found my way backstage to the entrance.

Standing behind the curtain, I could hear the people singing and praising the Lord. In my hand was the same little accordion I had used to lift the spirits of the downcast people in the neighborhood of San Francisco years ago.

"You know I'll never be able to go out there again," I sighed to the Lord. "I just can't do it."

Then I was overwhelmed by quiet words of encouragement.

"Marilynn, don't forget that I'm your Lord, the Alpha and the Omega, the Beginning and the End. Trust me. Pick up the accordion. Go out there and I'll sing through you."

Filling my lungs with a breath of fresh air and inspiration, I walked out on stage to sing. The song the Lord placed in my heart was "The Joy of the Lord is My Strength." As I began to sing, I felt the entire mass of worried confusion break up and flow out of me. It was almost as if I had crushed my cares into tiny crumbs and scattered them over the whole audience. While bearing one another's burdens, twelve hundred people can smile at something which would destroy an individual. This catharsis of music, prayer, and fellowship reassured me beyond any doubt that God was faithful to his promises. Truly, he would not try me above what I was able to endure.

Later that evening, I went back to my mother's place to pick up Kim. Instead of finding a broken rag doll of doubt and sorrow, I picked up a smiling, enthusiastic teen. She was jumping and shouting and showing me the projects she and Grandma Roberts had done while I was gone. Kim came home and never again showed signs of sorrow externally.

I know there was a scar, because she withdrew from some of the outward signs of affection and hugs we shared so freely before that night. But, in her determination, she said to herself, "My other friends have moms and dads who have been divorced, and they get by. Somehow, I can, too."

In some ways we became even more bonded together. In our determination, Kim and I began to do a great deal of searching for family activities we could do to restore ourselves. For the first time we discovered how much fun it was to go camping. Those quiet nights together helped rebuild our confidence and encourage our soul mending.

My brother-in-law, John Kramar, was our landlord. He allowed me to put in a swimming pool. Here was a safe way to drown our sorrows and burn off some energy.

We shared through vacations and special moments where we tried to help each other get over the crest of this crisis. Kim and I will always remember those special times of camping, swimming, and other outings.

MARK WAS ANOTHER STORY

This young man who was supposed to "take care of his mom and his sister" was unable to take care of himself.

Mark was uncontrollable. Though he still lived at home, this unfortunate sixteen-year-old was bent on self destruction. He skipped school so much that they finally expelled him. He was caught stealing on a number of occasions.

One time Kim came home from junior high school and reported, "Guess what, Mom? Someone stole my flute from the band room. In fact, they stole all the instruments."

A few weeks later, the police knocked on our door and asked for permission to "check up on some reports we have about your son." In the attic of our garage, they found all of the school's musical instruments. Mark was placed on probation for that incident.

Later he served time in jail for drug possession.

At the age of nineteen, he married a beautiful Korean girl. Her mom had left her when she was five, so she immediately accepted me as a mother. I loved her as my own. She was the same age as Kim.

Soon after their marriage, Mark left for the Navy. While his wife Jin was carrying their baby, he was carrying on with a dreadful drug and alcohol habit, which included PCP and other powerful, mind-altering drugs. Each day went from bad to worse. One day some type of chemical mixed with paint fumes on deck and sent him out of his mind. They tell me it took eight to ten men to hold him down. Mark was admitted to a psychiatric hospital in Hawaii.

Meanwhile, his young wife was making a happy home for herself with me in California. But it didn't last.

Upon release Mark came home with an honorable discharge. But the former sailor was a personal shipwreck. He couldn't handle a job, and he couldn't handle his marriage.

The turmoil and personal conflict were so intense that it

became evident that Mark's wife, now pregnant, was going to have to do something to protect her unborn child. I did everything I could to help her. We even called a priest who was a close friend of the family to conduct a special Mass for the unborn child asking the Lord's blessing and healing.

One day I received a call telling me that Jin had been rushed to the hospital, and it was probable that the baby would be born prematurely. We knew that at six months the child had little chance for survival. The doctors had told her that because of the undue stress, she was about to deliver prematurely.

As I spoke with her, I opened my heart and we shared this sorrowful moment together. She confided that she might have to leave and try to find help if she was going to save this baby's life. She wanted with all her being to give birth to this baby and to have the child born in peace.

Fortunately, Jin was able to leave and have her baby in peace—a healthy baby boy whom Jin and Mark named Sean. Since Jin and Mark got a divorce at the time of Sean's birth and Jin was granted custody of Sean, this little one was spared from suffering the consequences of his father's addiction. For that, I am eternally grateful.

AWESOME TIMES OF SWEEPING EMOTION

These were awesome times of sweeping emotion in my life. They might have swept me completely away if I had not been rooted in the Lord.

I thought back on those days in Colombia which had brought a great deal of sunshine and joy into my life. It is only natural that a little rain must fall. And when surmounted, I reminded myself, times of testing can do nothing but make you a stronger person. I would learn much more about that truth later.

Through it all, I knew on that first night when I gave my

life to the Lord at the age of fourteen that I would never, ever stop. But I confess I never realized I would have to go through anything like these trying times.

With my broken heart, all I could do was humble myself to the point of a personal death in Christ. Watching Glenn walk out with another woman; watching Mark incapable of serving as husband to his wife or father to his unborn child—these events taught me what it meant to die. Something perished deep inside of me. I learned that you can't trust your own resources or strength. I was learning to live totally dependent upon the power of the cross of Jesus Christ.

Where before I lived knowing that I had great favors given to me by the Lord, I had never before learned how to depend totally upon him. When that realization comes, it changes your life. I know because it changed mine.

Now I could begin to understand the perspective of the sorrowful Lord and his sorrowful mother, the Virgin Mary. Anyone can understand, on some level, why Mary sang at the moment of the annunciation, proclaiming the miraculous virgin birth of the Savior. But only those who have been tried and tested by the Lord can understand why she could still sing, "My soul doth magnify the Lord" at the foot of the cross. This holy woman knew who she was and why she had been created. Out of that commitment came strength and acceptance to see her through the death of her son.

Convictions such as these helped grind up and mix the apothecary that would mend my soul and effect lasting reconciliation.

SIX

Reconciliation

THE PROBLEMS WERE HERE TO STAY. But that didn't mean I couldn't move beyond them.

Four or five years after Mark's serious drug troubles began, I finally awakened to the concept of codependency. When Mark was about twenty-three, I started attending Al-Anon meetings. These are designed by the same people who formed Alcoholics Anonymous and are intended for the family members of an addict. At these meetings, I began to discover my own suffering and sickness. The more I could overcome this sickness in myself, the more I could help Mark.

Al-Anon taught me the meaning of codependency. It's difficult for someone who comes out of a ministerial family to concede that Jesus won't solve every problem with a wave of his hand. He has the answers, but we often forget that he intends for us to work out the details.

Al-Anon taught me the hard lesson that if someone in your home has a problem with alcoholism or any other addiction, you are likely to be sick also. I began to see that I was enveloped in Mark's sickness.

Still I thought the Lordship of Jesus Christ and the power of the Spirit could get us out of whatever sickness or problem might come along. I felt it would be pretty easy.

What I didn't realize was that Christ is not always eager to get us out of a problem we *don't want to acknowledge.*

Now through my divorce and family problems, I was beginning to realize I wasn't so powerful after all. As someone who was involved in Mark's life of alcoholism, I was almost as sick as he was. With God's grace, I had to do something to change myself in order to break the cycle of dependency.

As a mother of an addicted child and as the leader of a nurturing organization, I began to realize how much I needed nurturing myself. I began to recognize my own needs for help.

Esther encouraged me to go to Al-Anon. She and I came to listen. People were relating the mistakes they had made with the alcohol abusers in their families. What we heard began to sound all too familiar.

These wives and mothers were bailing out their children every time they needed a dollar. They accepted them back no matter how much verbal abuse was involved. They simply accepted the fact that this family member was entitled to abuse them and their family because of alcoholism. No one had authority over the situation. Poor them.

Poor us! Here was a litany of all the ways I was continuing to enable this terrible sickness in my family. I immediately identified with the problem and wanted help in correcting things.

I didn't have to attend very often, because it was only a matter of a few weeks until I began to catch on to the fact that this old girl was going to have to make definite decisions concerning this situation. This was the same realization I had reached before in regard to our earlier family crisis with Glenn. At that time, we at the Mission asked the Lord to take charge and solve the problem. Now I was going to have to do the same sort of thing with Mark, even if it meant he might never speak to me again. All that really mattered was for me to personally step in and change my attitude toward these problems.

Al-Anon releases you from the feelings of guilt. A mother's natural instinct is to save her child. Substance abusers know exactly how to play these feelings to get what they want. What I needed was "permission" to deny Mark the things that would hurt him. No more loans. No more cars (since he'd almost ruined the Mission's vehicle). No more pity for being alone with these problems apart from his father. I came to realize that each one of us has a will of his or her own.

A lot of mothers come to me and say, "I can relate to you because my son is an alcoholic." Sometimes they begin to cry, or they begin to say, "Please help me. Pray for my alcoholic son because he is living at home and tearing our life apart. Pray that he might be healed."

I want to cry out, "Awake! Wake up and realize that your child has the power to decide to continue living in this sickness, or he or she can make a definite decision to humbly ask for help. But you have to make that decision, too. You can't allow your own life to become more and more enveloped in your loved one's sickness. You have to wake up to the fact that it's not as easy as saying, 'Pray for him,' because you have to first recognize the sickness in yourself."

The wisdom I gained from Al-Anon fit in perfectly with my understanding of the gospel. The program is made up of twelve steps. But the first is one of the most important: everyone has to recognize that he can do nothing on his own power to save himself. Only a greater power, God's power, can heal him of his disease. But his first step has to be to humble himself, to recognize that he cannot do it alone.

That's an experience tied very closely to the gospel: we preach salvation based on the fact that we have all sinned and separated ourselves from God's life within us. Our first step toward reconciliation is to humble ourselves and confess our sins. God is faithful and just to forgive and to cleanse us from all unrighteousness. But the first step is to admit that we can do nothing about our problems on our own and to admit that we need help.

KIM HAS ENOUGH

Throughout these busy years, Kim was involved with her schoolwork and job at CharisMissions. She and I were drawing closer. As time went by, she began to open herself more and talk honestly with me about her feelings. She, too, was saddened over her brother's problems. But I am sure she had buried herself in her own world, trying to escape the harsh reality of it all. That is, until she had had enough.

Several years ago Mark went on a cocaine run for 17 days. He was going down the tubes—a mere skeleton. He would regularly come home and fill the air with blasphemy, demolishing me verbally with his uncontrolled anger and hostility.

One day while he was hurling epithets and venting his anger at me, Kim happened to stop in. She had recently had a heart-to-heart talk with Esther which caused a most atypical reaction toward her older and bigger brother.

"You know, I've got something to tell you and you won't believe it. But you can't tell my mom. I've always wanted to tell you . . ."

Kim went on to relate how she had experimented with drugs at one time. She was by no means an addict, but she had for a time been involved with drugs, little to her mother's knowledge.

"I thought I was going to die," she related to Esther. "And from that day on I quit cold turkey. I never wanted to go near the stuff again."

"You're still going to have to tell your mom," Esther advised. "You know, your mom isn't surprised at anything. You should tell her."

Fortunately, Kim was being called into her own conversion experience and had decided to share this with me before that eventful day with Mark. I'm glad she had because this confession gave her the confidence she needed to confront her brother.

While Mark was gushing out his anger and hate toward me, his little sister boldly thrust herself into the middle of the fray. Mind you, Kim was the "little sister" who had never before stood up to him or given him a moment's pain in her life.

"Mark, you'll never in this house again talk to your mom like this. So help me God, we've gone through the same experiences. We've shared life together. We have the same parents. We've been hurt. We've been raised in the same house. I know you are hurting, but I want to tell you, you will never ever talk like this to my mom in this house again!"

Her conviction and sincerity stopped Mark for a moment, but only a moment.

A few times in his life, I have seen Mark attack someone physically. This was one of the more memorable ones.

He grabbed his sister by the arm and pushed her against the wall. Then he put his hands on her neck. Before I could react and pull him off, Kim threw him back. She did so with remarkable strength and sternly proclaimed, "You can kill me if you want to, but before you touch me again, I have something to tell you. Will you sit down and listen?"

To my surprise, he sat down and gave her an audience. Kim proceeded to tell him the whole testimony of her life, right there on the spot. She related all their years together; our missionary life and the experience of our family life; our pain and our sorrow; our joys.

"Your only hope is to get help. You've got to die to yourself before you die by yourself. You can't do it alone. Look at yourself. You're dying right now, Mark. You don't have many days to live. Please, listen to us and tell me that you'll get help."

Mark's brain was wired on coke that afternoon, but somehow Kim's message sank through. Suddenly he broke down and cried.

"Please, Sis, help me."

Kim got on the phone. Within an hour she had his insurance papers all worked up, and that very afternoon Mark was off to a drug treatment program in Long Beach.

This experience caused us as a family to come together and to begin dealing with our codependency in the midst of these horrendous problems.

This renewed and motivated young woman reminded me of the prophecy my mother proclaimed the night before our first departure for Colombia as Pentecostal missionaries, "You shall have many daughters in Israel." Kim is but one daughter in the church. But she is also a living reminder to me of the thousands of new Esthers God is calling through CharisMissions.

All of God's believers are called to become children in his family. Daughters are that special form of child with the capacity to bring new life into the world. I see myself guiding a ministry that brings many daughters into the church who themselves birth new children in the Lord for the Father of us all. That prophecy from several decades ago is only now beginning to manifest itself through my calling. This fruit will endure because it is for the kingdom of God.

PUTTING BACK THE PIECES AS A FAMILY

The four of us, including Glenn, gathered regularly for family conferences during the time of Mark's drug treatment program to work out some of our problems. One night we were all going around the room in a small circle, letting everyone share personal feelings about the others.

Mark started screaming out to his dad, "I hate you, I hate you, I hate you" over and over again. This went on long enough to alarm us all. Suddenly, Mark broke down and cried. Something inside of him finally clicked because when he finished, he grabbed Glenn saying, "Dad, I have to tell you, I love you, I love you, I love you."

This had a profound effect on Glenn. As tears filled his eyes, he wrapped us all in his arms. We were all sobbing. I think we moved the whole room. He held on and wouldn't let go. From that time forward, we began to work as a family every week with Mark.

During Christmas of 1987, I finally worked up the courage to invite Glenn and his new wife over for a family meal. Much to my surprise, we had a happy holiday together. That broke down a great number of barriers.

Kim asked her father to help her at the next *Encuentro Latino*. He agreed.

Before one of the gatherings, he sat with me in the dressing room exchanging small talk. Then, without warning he walked over, hugged me, and said, "I love you; I always will. You're a great lady." This filled me with a deep sense of satisfaction and contentment.

He walked me to the platform, hugged me again, and said, "I'm so proud of you. Thank God for your faithfulness." He kissed me good-bye and left.

It hasn't all been easy, but my life has been restored in fullness. One unexpected occasion of freedom came the day my marriage was officially anulled by the Catholic church, confirming even more the vocation God has given me, to spend myself in the work of evangelization.

I had always said that Glenn's diploma from seminary was also mine. But I recognized that our greatest award in life is the Lord himself! This reality was confirmed in May 1978 when Franciscan University of Steubenville, Ohio, bestowed on me an Honorary Doctorate in Humanities for the many years I have ministered to Hispanics. The Lord used this occasion to help me understand the he always affirms and confirms his calling in our lives—in his time and in his way.

RETURN TO THE ASSEMBLIES OF GOD?

People ask me if I could ever return to the Assemblies of God. I could never return—because truly I have never left. Now I know what it is to live in the heart of the church. I can serve all of my brothers and sisters with an ecumenical heart. I have nothing to lose, and I have no desire to return to the past. "Forgetting the past and looking forward to what lies ahead, I strain to reach the end of the race and receive the prize for which God is calling me..." (Phil 3:14).

I will always treasure my background in the Assemblies of God. It helped prepare me for my present work of evangelization. My ability to design programs, my life in the Spirit, my zeal to follow Christ, my enthusiasm for world missions, my desire to proclaim the Good News—all these gifts and abilities were developed and rooted in me while I was still a child. I came to a living faith, a vibrant relationship with Jesus Christ and with his body.

In addition, I have now discovered something more. Through the sacramental life and teaching of the Catholic church, the Holy Spirit has given me a greater understanding of the fullness of his truth. I don't believe any of us truly lives in the fullness of all God has prepared for those who love him. There is always more.

But we cannot even begin to discover what God has prepared for us without opening his gifts. The areas of Christian faith I experienced in the Assemblies of God churches were not all that God had prepared for me. Through these gifts, the Lord has empowered me. I am now equipped to move ahead in the work of evangelization that he has entrusted to me. God has truly given me a promising future.

SEVEN

A Promising Future

I AM GRATEFUL FOR THE WORK OF reconciliation that has begun in my family. I am amazed at what God is doing, through my brokenness and dying, for my family and for the ministry of CharisMissions. One day I was walking through our Porciuncula Center—the largest service center in the United States, both in budget and facilities, for the work of Catholic evangelization and charismatic renewal services. All of this has been purchased and paid for by immigrating Spanish-speaking participants in the life of CharisMissions ministries.

This is an impossible dream come true, a place of our own, offices where more than thirty full-time employees work for the operations of CharisMissions throughout the world. It's a place where more than two thousand Spanish-speaking people come weekly to be nourished and formed, and are then sent out for the work of evangelization and renewal.

It all seems to come before me, like a vision, this great work of the Lord, for which I am extremely grateful and much humbled. I can't help but think of the more than ten thousand people each month who directly receive the ministries of evangelization and renewal through the famiy of CharisMissions; of the many missions, campaigns, rallies, courses, and seminars that are offered both by adult and family ministries, including youth ministries and children's ministries.

I think of the plays being written and directed, of the music being composed and then skillfully and professionally recorded by CharisMissions members, of the liturgical ministries and prayer and intercession teams serving the needs of the people.

I see the thousands of tapes, books, publications, and videotapes that are distributed from our offices. I see over one thousand volunteers that serve faithfully in the hundreds of evangelization events each year offered by CharisMissions. I praise God for allowing me as general advisor for the Spanish-speaking prayer groups to be able to serve over two hundred of these groups in the Archdiocese of Los Angeles alone. It has been a joy to watch these prayer groups grow, live, and serve the renewal through their parishes.

I see the television studio for the half-hour weekly television program called "Alabaré," which proclaims the gospel on the largest Spanish-language television station in Los Angeles, as well as other major cities in the United States and Latin America. This program has boldly proclaimed the power of Jesus as Lord and uses many gifted people to spread the Word. God has helped us to hold the number one rating on the Sunday morning slot in the Los Angeles area for many months now.

I think of the annual *Encuentro Latino* and the more than sixteen thousand people who traveled from all over the United States and throughout Latin America to attend this year's convention. More than one hundred priests attended the special two-day retreat before the convention. The Institute of Proclaimers, an evangelization school, was offered at the close of the convention.

I feel so humbled seeing more than fifty youth evangelists who are in formation to preach as lay Catholic men and women in the church. I see the joy on the faces of many seminarians who have felt the call to the priesthood through CharisMissions ministries. I am especially thankful for the many Hispanic seminarians now studying for the priesthood as a result of their contact with the Mission.

I see the little children who have been born from the broken families of immigrants—families that are struggling to survive here in the United States. I see them take the microphones to sing and lead the people in praise and worship. I see parents who had lived through child abuse, alcoholism, witchcraft, and sickness come forth. I see them take leading roles among our forty coordinators of ministries in the CharisMissions society as well as the prayer group ministry.

I see how young people from the streets lead more than two thousand youth to Christ each month through rallies and evangelization missions. I am thrilled that they have developed to the point where more than five thousand youth will gather soon for their own annual *Encuentro Latino*.

I feel a strong arm of protection through CharisMissions' board of directors and especially Msgr. Alfred Hernandez, liaison with the archdiocese for CharisMissions Missionary Society and prayer group ministries. He has so faithfully walked with me since Msgr. Montrose's appointment as bishop of Stockton, California. I praise God for also allowing me to serve as a member on the United States Catholic Bishops' Ad Hoc Committee for Evangelization. In particular, I am grateful for my wonderful friendships with various bishops and, of course, Fr. Anastacio Rivera, the Hispanic Director of the Archdiocese of Los Angeles. I am also grateful for the many priest advisors, who with their love and pastoral concerns helped me to continue in the ministry of evangelization.

I could go on and on, and we will. We will continue to stretch ourselves, strive for larger facilities, and greater potential in preaching and teaching. We will proclaim the Word through the radio and television networks and by all scientific means possible. We will create a new sound and make use of the printed page even more. The charismatic renewal ministries work in parishes will give life and hope to our churches. This will all be for the glory of God. In the words of St. Paul: "Eye has not seen, ear has not heard, neither has it entered into the heart of man the things that God has prepared for those who love him" (1 Cor 2:9).

TRUSTING GOD IN YOUR BROKENNESS

Considering the work of CharisMissions as it is today, I know I couldn't have pastored this people if I hadn't suffered a broken heart. Most likely, I would always have seen myself as above that type of brokenness. I came close to the brokenness of others in the barrio of San Francisco in Cartagena and on the streets of Los Angeles. I wasn't afraid of the condition of those I encountered, but I had never truly experienced it until those days of darkness with Glenn, Mark, and Kim. "Weeping may go on all night, but in the morning there is joy" (Ps 30:5). If you live in the life of the Spirit and trust in Jesus Christ and seek to cultivate his virtues, you are always going to experience peace and joy in the end. Somehow it's going to happen in God's time. You walk one day at a time.

"Honey," my mom always said, "as long as you have hope, your eyes will always be open." Yes, the Lord will always give you the inclination of his heart to know how to continue searching for peace and joy.

That doesn't mean that I believe the way we lived before will ever be possible again. After our failures, God rarely puts us back in the same situation again. God draws straight through crooked lines. At times we don't know where our lives are leading, but we do know that as long as we keep our eyes open and continue to live in his heart, he puts everything right in the end.

THE GIFTEDNESS OF ALL OUR
BROTHERS AND SISTERS IN CHRIST

If you asked me to share some of my dreams, one of them would be to see our Catholic believers look at fellow brothers and sisters in Christ with the eyes of Jesus and to discover their giftedness and their participation in the body of Christ. I believe we can always see people in one of two ways, as a potential for good or as a problem. Through our prejudices or preconceived ideas, or possibly our bad experiences, we tend to judge others. This, to my way of thinking, paralyzes the body of Christ.

We need to understand the giftedness of others in order to appreciate and respect them. This will help us see how God's accomplishments in the lives of others relate to our experience within the Catholic church.

I favor honest openness and exchange between denominations, but exchange with awareness. I become uneasy when I hear people say, "Well, let's go visit one of their assemblies, or let's go to their church." Someone might visit some other church and experience a lot of wonderful things: beauty in worship and fellowship in ways that may be missing in his or her own life. Then the person might think, "Gee, this church must be better than mine because this really makes me feel good. The way they sing, the way they pray, the way they fellowship together, the way their children are instructed. What am I missing in my own church family?"

I feel Catholics should examine the giftedness within their own household and be evangelized thoroughly enough to understand their own values, their own beauty, their own worth. Then when we search for unity with Protestant brothers and sisters, we can go secure in our own identity. In this way we begin to discover not only the gifts in the lives of our brothers and sisters, but also the gifts in our own lives.

Honest ecumenism is more than attending another

church's service. It's basically a matter of being transparent to brothers and sisters of other traditions, not seeing them as threats, but seeing them as lessons and blessings.

In turn, I think Protestants are going to have to risk accepting the fact that their Catholic brothers and sisters are a part of the body of Christ. They need to listen and be willing to accept the giftedness and the beauty that we Catholic people bring. It is possible for Protestants to develop personal relationships with Catholics just as I experienced it in Colombia with the Carmelite Missionary Sisters. We are all formed to live a life of faith. This can be enjoyable and productive for both sides.

Imagine a retreat of Catholics and Protestants who want to evangelize together! It's not only the Catholics who go to the Protestants and say, "We're one in Jesus, let's go tell the people that we love him." But the Protestant brothers and sisters also need to be willing to accept how Catholic believers came to that realization in the first place. The story may be different from what they expected to hear. Both groups may be surprised to learn how faith comes by hearing and how we have personally heard and received the Word of God in different ways.

Recently, we examined this in a retreat together. As Catholics and Protestants, we shared the giftedness that brought us to the reality of our relationship with Jesus. It was interesting to hear the Protestant women telling about how they felt the gift of faith come to them through programs in their church. They memorized the Scripture, sang choruses, and enjoyed all kinds of personal programs in their church. On the other hand, the Catholic women told how their gift of faith came to life through baptism, praying the Rosary by the side of their Grandma, or through their First Communion. The manner in which a Catholic comes to the heart of Jesus can differ from the manner in which a

Protestant comes. But life in Jesus is the same. We have to be willing to reach beyond our prejudices to discover what these experiences mean to each one of us.

OVERCOMING THE PREJUDICE

Some believers are imprisoned by walls of prejudice. It is sad to see that even the mere mention of the word "Mary" causes many Protestants to get defensive. By the same token, Catholics can get defensive when certain Christians ask, "Are you saved?" or lead off a statement with, "But the Bible says..."

I don't think we can foster harmony by proclaiming a solitary doctrine, belief, or particular theology. Basically I think we begin on the level of friendship. A friend isn't a friend without a willingness to listen and to receive, in honesty, the heart of the other.

Some people hold preconceived ideas about what they seek in these cross-denominational exchanges. But it doesn't work that way. It has to happen naturally. All of a sudden you may discover that Jesus is there at the center of that relationship, filling it with his happiness, joy, and peace. From there, you can naturally share the testimony of your life in Christ with your friend.

People want to know where I've been, where I've come from, how I have found my new life in Christ, and where it's taking me now. I can share that with anyone without shame.

Catholics are often afraid to do this because they assume Protestants are much more skillful at presenting their life testimony. But more than a spoken testimony is required. Life is to be shared. And when you begin to share your life with others, you're much closer to sharing the true joys, sorrows, and glories of Jesus.

BE CONFIDENT ABOUT YOUR FAITH

Are you confident about the foundations of your faith? It's no longer safe to simply drift along with the crowd and assume the church of your parents will become the church of your children. It's not even safe to assume the church of your parents will, through baptism alone, remain the church of your salvation.

Today God is moving in powerful ways through the lives of Catholics and Protestants alike. Are you prepared to stand before a renewed, enthusiastic, and deeply converted Protestant and share with this believer the giftedness of your own faith? Or have you allowed your spiritual gifts to burn down to a cold ember?

Life is too fraught with sexual pulls, temptations, and violence for us to seek shelter behind a papier-mâché religion. Such a facade may look great, but withstands nothing. We need solid foundations of faith, walls of deeds, and roofs of conviction to house us. These can't be built through hollow ritualism or assumed religiosity. They must be constructed through renewal and a sincere life lived out in the power of Christ's love.

As your greatest enemy, Satan is extremely deceitful. He can trick you into believing a lukewarm "form" of godliness is all you need to survive. Then you're at the mercy of anyone who comes along proclaiming the false joys of godlessness.

I feel that I am a living testimony to the power of God's mercy, and his power to restore and renew. As an Assemblies of God missionary, I walked into the Carmelite convent in Cartagena to "convert" the nuns. But I hadn't counted on the strength of their gifts to recognize the strength of mine.

Fr. O'Callaghan dared to pit his "whole pie" against my "full gospel." Hundreds of parishioners in Latin America and Southern California fueled the fires of renewal with their love for the Spirit. These humble believers attracted me to the Catholic church.

Without the strength of God's promises, I could not have survived life without Glenn, the sorrow of my son's chemical dependency, or the weight of this ministry. How much are you willing to endure without the Rock and Fortress of Jesus' presence in your life?

Through the pages of this book, I have tried to take off the mask of vanity and self-deception and share the real Marilynn Kramar with you. I hope you can do the same with yourself as well.

My God is able to save your life from ruin. If you let him do it, joy will come in the morning!

EPILOGUE

The Treasures of the Faith

THE STORY OF MY LIFE CONTINUES to be centered in Christ and his mission in this world. The Lord has called me to serve him through the Catholic faith. The more I meditate on this reality the more I realize it is full of treasures that God has made available to us. As Catholic believers, we should look for and appropriate this grace in our lives.

In this epilogue, I want to share with you the grace that I have personally found in the heart of the church and how much it has helped me in my personal life.

Losing my husband and spiritual coworker at the same time was a devastating blow. I knew I needed help and, fortunately, I knew where to find it. I don't know what I would have done if I hadn't been a believer.

THE HIERARCHY: A STRENGTH AND PROTECTION

One great strength of the church is the spiritual protection and direction the hierarchy provides. Some people are afraid to open this door. They don't want to confront the powers that be for fear of being told what to do. In my case, I have discovered that instead of limiting us, the hierarchy is there to protect and free us.

Perhaps my perspective is different than that of most people because I came out of a leadership position within the Assemblies of God church. Growing up in the home of a pastor made it much easier for me to approach people in church leadership, whether Protestants or Catholics.

But the leadership and covering of the church is one of its greatest gifts. Those who shy away from this power deny themselves a vast arsenal of strength, especially when they are confused or troubled and in need of guidance.

I find great comfort in the promises from the documents of Vatican II. In the "Dogmatic Constitution on the Church," the council fathers speak of the mystery of the church saying, "The Holy Spirit guides the Church into the fullness of all truth and gives her a unity of fellowship and service. He furnishes and directs her with various gifts both hierarchical and charismatic," . . . (ch. 1, no. 4).

Knowing that I am part of the church and because of that I am blessed with both grace (*charis*), which is a work of the Spirit, and am part of the body of Christ, a structured and ordered work of God, I must recognize the gift of the hierarchy to me. If there is a body without breath or movement, there is no life. But if there is movement without a body or a body without a head to order it, there is chaos.

In the turmoil and confusion of my situation, the need for the covering and protection of the hierarchy became very clear. Immediately after Glenn left, I made an appointment with Cardinal Manning. I brought everything that made up the Mission: the constitution, bylaws, accounting records—literally everything—and laid it at his feet. I was determined to give it over to the Lord by submitting it to my shepherd for his discernment and direction. This wasn't out of obligation. It was out of an earnest desire to be certain that God was in charge of my life. I needed and expected that reassurance. I had never walked through the chancery door and been disappointed.

After I'd unburdened myself, the cardinal took me by the hand and said, "Girl, you can't quit. You have to promise me you'll keep going. Can't you see the grace of the church falling on you?"

The Treasures of the Faith / 145

"Cardinal Manning, I can't do it alone. I have to have a covering. I can't stand it by myself like this."

"Don't worry," he reassured. "Within two weeks I'll have an answer for you."

That was all he said. That was all I needed him to say. So I left.

Then two weeks later a letter arrived, assigning Msgr. Donald Montrose of Resurrection Parish, now bishop of Stockton, California to me. A torrent of grateful thoughts poured through my mind: "Donald Montrose was a bilingual pastor, a wonderful friend, and former director of education in the Department of Education in the archdiocese. He had been an inspiration to me in the renewal. Now he was assigned to me as my covering, and he was committed to walk through this with me. Here was one of the finest sources of encouragement I could have received.

The door to his office was always open to me, but he seldom wanted to stay in that formal setting. More often than not, he would say, "Marilynn, let's go out and have some breakfast." We consumed a great number of *huevos rancheros* at a small Mexican restaurant nearby. Throughout our meetings, he expressed a strong desire to nurture my plans in the Lord for CharisMissions.

Msgr. Montrose was a great listener. He was an American whose whole life was enveloped in serving the poor and simple folk of Latin America. He didn't perform any dramatic breakthrough for me, but he was always there guiding, steering, and providing the protection I needed to keep my fledgling ministry alive. Though extremely busy, he would sit for hours on end drawing out my ideas with attentive nods. I felt the secure arm of a father giving silent reassurance, as though he were saying, "We'll walk through this together."

Around the time of these meetings with Msgr. Montrose, the divorce became final. And Glenn was asking the church for an annulment of our marriage. In the Catholic faith, we do not believe in divorce as such, but we do have a process of annulment.

By much investigation and dialogue, the marriage tribunal in a particular diocese discerns *if* a particular marriage was from its beginning a true and compatible union in Christ. They discern whether certain impediments or obstacles were present at the time of the marriage, which would be cause for annulment. If so, the annulment is granted.

In the midst of my pain, I had always said that I would fight for my rights. No one would annul my marriage. But the day of my interview with the marriage tribunal for the Archdiocese of Los Angeles happened to fall on the feast of Our Lady of Guadelupe, Patroness of Evangelization.

I remember sitting in the car out in the parking lot, openly weeping. But soon my weeping became a submissive entreaty to our Blessed Mother. Through the tears, I begged, "Take me to Jesus. I will not fight for my rights. I give my life into your hands. Pray for your daughter. Wrap her in your arms and ask Jesus to give her his answer."

Our marriage was unanimously annulled. This decision brought me to a fuller realization of the power of discernment through church authority, showing how it gives us assurance and direction. More than ever before, I also became aware of my own vocation and purpose in life as an evangelizer, of Guadelupe.

COMMUNITY: THE BODY OF CHRIST IN ACTION

One of the greatest gifts for any Christian is the community of love: a sense of family. Like my father, a Pentecostal minister, beautifully put it so often, "Marilynn, you are so lucky to have a family."

My next source of support came from rediscovering the

strength of the people of CharisMissions—my own little Christian community. They buoyed me up, not because they felt sorry for me, but because they respected what God was doing through me in their own lives and families. They wanted me to continue, because all of them wanted to continue in this work of the Lord.

It was encouraging to see this community of evangelizers and staff who often felt self-conscious about themselves now walk shoulder to shoulder beside me. With God's grace, I had helped them overcome trials and live as victorious Christians. With a precious faith, they believed that God could do the same thing for me. How could I fail them?

During those dark days just after Glenn's departure, my Latino friends and supporters would come up and say, "We feel called to stand with you and help you." Others would tell me, "We need to pray together." Suddenly, as I was becoming a spiritual widow, numerous married couples came into my life unbidden. They were a great fountain of encouragement for me.

I began to discover many abilities I had which possibly had been suffocated or long forgotten. I felt responsible in the Lord for the CharisMissions family. I began to experience the gifts of knowledge and wisdom to see spiritually God's will for each day, and the know-how needed to "take steps" in the right direction. I asked for nothing more than strength and wisdom for the day.

I awakened to the reality of my giftedness in administration as well as in preaching and teaching. Through the encouragement of friends and supporters, I began to see myself in a new light and to see in a new way the potential of others in our work.

The actual departments of CharisMissions remained intact, just as Glenn and I had perceived them together, but day by day they were stretched, augmented, and multiplied.

THE EUCHARIST: MY GREATEST RESERVOIR OF STRENGTH

I know from experience that our safest protection in times of trouble is in our faith. There we are at the heart of the church. This is especially true in the Eucharist, where Christ re-presents the perfect and acceptable sacrifice of himself to the Father for our salvation. For me this is the greatest reservoir of strength.

During the Mass, it isn't necessary for anyone to sing or clap hands or dance. I'm face-to-face with Jesus at the altar. There I can lay down my own life as an offering through his Body and his Blood. At times like this, it isn't enough to simply hear sermons about the "Power of the Blood." They must be applied!

When Jesus held up the meager offering of the little boy—the one that fed five thousand people in the wilderness—he asked his Father to bless it. He then miraculously broke the bread and distributed the loaves and fish to the multitudes, and they had their fill. That is the essence of the Mass. When we understand the mystery of the Body and Blood of Christ, we find our greatest strength.

Our life becomes the offering that is consecrated through the Body and Blood of Jesus. Christ offers us to the Father. We are not only blessed, but enveloped in him. Jesus converts us into his very Body, into his life. We are then allowed to be broken as he desires and permits. Then we are shared with the whole world along with all of the elements—the other brothers and sisters who are part of his Body.

This understanding doesn't come easily. In recent months I was pleased to hear Kim, now twenty-five, relate the one concept that kindled her interest in Mass. "You go through this period where you go to church because you have to every Sunday. I would follow the sit-kneel-stand, sit-kneel-stand routine and say the things I was supposed to say. For a long time that's all it was to me. I would sit there at the homily and receive the message, which I usually felt wasn't as good as the Protestant sermons I remembered. Receiving the Eucharist didn't seem that important.

"Then one day it came to me that the real part of the Mass wasn't to receive, but it's to *give* myself. When I realized that, that's when it became very powerful."

Certainly, I'm elated that Kim has such an understanding from the Lord. I feel invincible when I approach the Mass with that kind of expectation. We speak of this moment as the "Glorious Offering." No human being could give this gift to me. Few are the sermons that can impart such inspiration. People ask me if I miss the good sermons given in Protestant churches. Truly it makes no sense to compare the effect that a good sermon has with the effect the Mass has. A sermon given in the power of the Holy Spirit can help people very much. But during the Mass something else takes place. If you understand the essence of the Mass, at the altar you will be transformed from death into life.

MARY, OUR MOTHER

Where there is a family, there is always a mother. I believe one of the subtle attacks of the enemy today is to destroy "family life." The strategy is to divide and separate not only the children, but also the mother, the father, and all relationships.

This also takes place in our Christian family. To say we do not need Mary is to say to Jesus, "I love you, but I don't want and I don't like your mom." Mary is an instrument, the model in the Holy Spirit who leads us to her Son, Jesus.

I can't fathom how we would think we are a family without Mama! What would my own children do without me? What would Jesus have done without Mary? When we are children, we are very dependent on Mama. When we are teenagers, we think we can live without her. When we become adults, we return to wrap her in our arms and tell her, "What would I ever have done without you?"

In our childlike nature, which Jesus speaks of so often and teaches so much about, we learn to love Mary. That's what my own parents taught me to do, even given their evangelical, Pentecostal background. As teenagers, as such in the renewal, at times we feel we can get along without Mama. We wish she "wasn't at home." As mature Christians, we receive her as St. John did at the foot of the cross and invite her into "our home."

Those of us who are mothers realize we've made many mistakes and even at times abused and tarnished the true image of what a mother should be. We've made it hard for our children to understand what a true Christian mom is or should be. This has happened also in the "Mother Church."

We as the church have often abused our dignity, sinned, committed errors, and thus caused Mary, our mother, to look less glorious than she really is. For this reason, many children have never seen her as she is. We need to repent of this and again to desire to know her in her rightful place where "she shall be called blessed for all generations" (Lk 1:48).

The mysteries of Jesus recalled through the Rosary signify the beauty of Mary leading us as children to the heart of Jesus through the Joyous, Sorrowful, and the Glorious Mysteries. I relate this to the Christian life as Dr. Robert Schuller expresses it: "In life you are nested, tested, and crested."

THE JOYFUL MYSTERIES OF THE ROSARY

The Joyful Mysteries of Jesus are experiences which all of us have in Jesus which "nest us." They give us the assurance of our salvation and our mission.

The Annunciation (Luke 1:26-38). As Mary listens to the Spirit of God through the angel Gabriel, she becomes aware

The Treasures of the Faith / 151

of God's will for her, of his confidence in her, his love for her. She trembles at the thought and wonders what this greeting means. She asks questions and needs signs, such as the words of confirmation regarding her cousin Elizabeth who had been sterile and was now pregnant with John the Baptist. Convinced and willing, she opens her life completely to the God she loves, desiring to be possessed only by him. Jesus is conceived in her womb by the power of the Holy Spirit.

This is my possibility, too, as I allow Jesus to be conceived in me. I desire to do his will and to be possessed by him alone.

Visitation (Luke 1:39-56). As Jesus is living within Mary's womb, being formed in her, she has a story to tell. She can't wait to give the good news to her cousin Elizabeth. She travels three days by donkey and by foot to see her. As the two cousins meet, Elizabeth has a special revelation from God about Mary and cries out, "Blessed are you among women and blessed is the fruit of your womb." In turn, Mary sings her praise to the Lord, "My being proclaims the greatness of the Lord and my spirit finds joy in God my savior."

I, too, have something to give. When I experience the meaning of "fiat"—giving my life totally to the Lord—he not only lives in me, but now I am able to give him to another.

Birth of Jesus (Luke 2:6-19). As Mary gives birth to Jesus in a lowly stable, I know that even in my humble, poverty-stricken stable, with the stench of the animals and the disasters that surround me, Jesus must be born. Thank God he wasn't born in a palace or in a perfect place. Then I would never have understood. I give birth to Jesus where I am, and he shines through the nothingness of my life, giving hope and great joy to me and to those that come to see him through my life.

Mary and Joseph Presenting Jesus in the Temple (Luke 2:22-40). Mary and Joseph present Jesus in the temple out of obedience. They return to offer Jesus to God the Father. An old man, Simeon, is about to die. He sees the child and his eyes are opened. Taking the child in his arms, he cries out, "I can die in peace. I have seen the Messiah." He then prophesies the future of the child and opens Joseph's and Mary's eyes to the reality of their own commitment. He prophesies to Mary with these words, "You see this child: he is destined for the fall and for the rising of many in Israel-destined to be a sign that is rejected; and a sword will pierce your own soul, too, so that the secret thoughts of many may be laid bare" (Lk 2:34-35).

I must be obedient as well to the commands of God. To be obedient I allow another to see Jesus. I present him in my "temple of clay." There are many Simeons who have closed their eyes hoping against hope to see the Messiah. As I am faithful, the Spirit reveals Jesus through me. Another sees him and then also participates in the life and mission of Jesus. Through another the prophetic word is given back to me, sometimes not as an easy word, but as real as the words spoken to Mary: "The sword will pierce your heart, so that the secret thoughts of many may be laid bare."

Jesus in the Temple (Luke 2:41-52). Mary and Joseph are in a frenzy realizing that Jesus has disappeared after they have taken him to Jerusalem to celebrate the Passover. He is only twelve years old, a mere boy. As he is found, he assures his mother that he has been in the temple all the time, fulfilling the will of his Father.

Many times I have also felt that Jesus has disappeared. I could not feel him near me. I could not touch him. But what a joy to find him in "my temple of clay." He tells me as he told Mary, "I've been here all the time doing the will of my Father." Even when I wasn't aware of it, he was working in my life and teaching me.

THE SORROWFUL MYSTERIES OF THE ROSARY

The Sorrowful Mysteries are those experiences of the passion of Jesus, the hard discipleship of the cross, the experiences that test my faith—the "testing."

The Scripture tells us that only the foolish man tries to build a tower without counting the cost. If I am nested in God and am living in the joy of my salvation, I will be tested. The Scripture says in Sirach 2:1, "My son, when you come to serve the Lord, prepare yourself for trials."

The Garden of Gethsemane or the Agony in the Garden (Matthew 26:36-38, Luke 22:41-44; Matthew 26:40-41). The Garden of Gethsemane is where Jesus cries out in loneliness. He takes upon his shoulders every lonely man and woman in the world. He confides that only the Father's will is what matters. He gives his human longings and expectations to the Father and cries, "Not my will, but thine be done."

In my own despair, when those I loved either left me, fell asleep, or just didn't care, I had to die to myself and carry my needs and theirs as well to God the Father. At my deepest hour of loneliness, I could only look to him and accept the strength of the Father's will for me.

Scourging at the Pillar (Mark 15:1-2; John 18:36-37; Luke 23:16, Isaiah. 53:5-7). Jesus is bent and torn for my sickness and pain. He is scourged and beaten for my suffering.

In giving my body up to him, I also take the human taunts and gibes that come my way, offering my life as a living sacrifice. I know that as I add my suffering to the suffering of Jesus, there will be salvation for many—not because of what I have done, but because of what he has accomplished in his passion and now wants to share with and through me.

Pope John Paul speaks of this human suffering in his

exhortation on suffering: "Suffering, as such, cannot be defined. It is a communion with" those for whom and those with whom we suffer.

Crowning with Thorns (Matthew 27:29; John 19:15). The soldiers took Jesus to the Praetorium, stripped him of his clothes, and dressed him in a purple robe. They put a crown of thorns upon his head and a branch in his right hand.

I also must unite my anguish with the body of Christ in all its suffering majesty. I know that all of my confusion and stress, the strain and the weight of my trials, is only another sign to me that Jesus wore his crown with dignity and was fully crowned by it. I receive strength in his kingly anguish to lift up my head knowing "from whence comes my help."

Invitation to Carry the Cross (Luke 9:23; Luke 23:11). Jesus tells us we cannot be his disciples if we are not willing to bear his cross. Jesus had to make the decision to carry it himself. No one could make that decision for him. He, by carrying it, took the "steps" necessary to reach Calvary to die for me and for you.

I am given this privilege, too. It is my choice to decide to take the steps and walk in his way! I cannot deviate from the road to Calvary. Some of my friends would try to convince me the cross is not necessary—that Jesus suffered once and for all and that now I must only live the life of the resurrected Lord.

This idea doesn't make sense to me. For if Jesus, the crossbearer, did not walk in my shoes, and I did not walk in his sandals, I would not now have any idea how to die to myself and take the steps needed to totally lay down my life for him.

The Crucifixion (Luke 23:46). The final breath of Jesus is the final struggle to give everything into the Father's hands. I have fought hard and long and so many times to do it *my* way: to try to demand *my* rights and protect *my* preconceived notion about *my* life and future.

It was only in the death of Jesus that the centurion's eyes were opened to truly see Jesus, the King of all kings. Only as I give up my own life and die to myself will another see the true Jesus as the "Lamb of God" who takes away the sins of the world. Jesus, have mercy upon me, a sinner!

THE GLORIOUS MYSTERIES OF THE ROSARY

As we pass through the valley of the shadow of death, the Lord is with us. Only in dying shall we be resurrected into new life—"crested."

Resurrection of Jesus (John 16:20-22; Luke 24:1; Matthew 28:2-8; John 11:25-26). As Jesus promised, "After three days I will rise again." He came forth triumphant from the grave and gives us the hope that if we have died with him, we will also rise with him.

Even now I can proclaim that Jesus is risen. How do I know? Because I have suffered and died with him. I know that no man, woman, son, daughter, or any circumstance of my life can keep me in the tomb. I have been tried and I have come forth victorious, a new creation.

Ascension of Jesus to Heaven (Matthew 28:18-20; Mark 16:9; Luke 24:50-51; Acts 1:9). Jesus ascends to heaven and prepares a place for me. As Jesus prayed at the Last Supper with his disciples before dying, he prays that he may return to his Father's side, having completed everything his Father sent him to do (Jn 17:4-8). As he ascends, the angels come to speak to the disciples gazing into the skies and tell them this same Jesus who has ascended will come again.

I know that as long as I do the will of my Father, I will one day be at complete rest. I will find fullness of joy in the place God has prepared for me. I know that I cannot keep on gazing into the sky. There is work for me to do. I must prepare for his coming. I know heaven awaits me, but I must occupy myself doing his will. I must also know my place here on earth and live my life doing what he has asked me to do.

Descent of the Holy Spirit—Pentecost (Acts 2:1-11). Jesus promised his disciples that as he returned to his Father, he would send them the Holy Spirit. He told them that as they received the Holy Spirit, they would become his witnesses unto the ends of the earth. Jesus was faithful as the baptizer in the Holy Spirit.

The fearful, forlorn disciples would never be the same again. On the day of Pentecost, the church—Christ's followers—was filled with the Spirit. The disciples were awakened and assured of their life and mission. They received not just one or two gifts, but all of his fullness, his virtues: the sacred gifts of his nature, the potential of the fruits of his Spirit, the charismatic gifts of the Spirit—those gifts that would move mountains and "confound the wise." Upon experiencing the promise of the Father, they went forth to fulfill Christ's mission in the power of the Holy Spirit.

Pentecost, to me, signifies the day of my awakening. It is the day when through obedience I realized that, even though I am a baptized Christian, I need to be awakened—shaken—as the bride of Christ and as a follower of Jesus. In myself I can do nothing, but I remember his promise to me: if I seek him and ask, he will send his grace, the power of his Spirit upon me, to fill me with love. He will give me the power to proclaim good news. He will allow me in Christ's love and zeal to minister and reach out to the world (my world), which has not yet known or accepted Jesus as Lord.

Assumption of Mary into Heaven (Song of Songs 2:10, 11, 14; Revelation 11:19, 12:1; Judith 13:23, 25; Judith 15:10). As our "Mother Church" teaches us, the Blessed Mother was assumed into heaven. As such, she entered into the joys of her Lord, not having to die, but being bodily lifted up to him, to be received by him.

I know that some might have a problem in believing this particular doctrine. But I believe that accepting Mary as my model gives me a clue of my own potential. I believe that from my baptism, from the day Jesus initiated me into his body, I am being lifted up to him. "From glory to glory," my body must rise.

My life must be headed in the direction of heaven. The joy of my salvation is knowing I am being assumed more and more into Christ's presence. I am, as are my fellow forerunners of faith, always looking toward heaven with my eye set firmly toward the mark of my "high calling" in Jesus Christ.

Coronation—The Crowning of Mary (Song of Solomon 2:1; Song of Solomon 6:10; Revelation 21:1-4). Mary, as she represents Mother Church, is not only assumed into heaven, but crowned by Jesus. He is the crowning. There awaits for me only one crown, Jesus, my Lord and my God. I know that if I will live and work as my Blessed Mother, Mary, did, I will receive my crown of joy and forever be with him in "glory."

I know that I must live out my Christian life as an authentic follower of Jesus. I know that each day and each hour is a challenge and an adventure as I walk in the joy, sorrow, and glory of Jesus Christ, my Lord. Thank God for a mother like Mary who walks beside me, teaching and leading me as her child in a closer walk with Jesus.

These are some of the convictions that held me up when all else was sinking beneath my feet. As I focused more on Christ within me and less on the failure around me, I gradually emerged from my despair.

As I examine how things are going, I see Glenn married to another woman and Mark still fighting for full recovery from drug abuse. But I no longer stand in the same place. Now I'm standing at the threshhold of reconciliation and hope. Conditions aren't perfect, but they press me onward toward Jesus and his kingdom, filled with great appreciation for the treasures of my Catholic faith.

How You Can Be Involved in the Work of CharisMissions

Yes, Marilynn, I am interested in the work of evangelization.

☐ Send me _____ copies of *The Marilynn Kramar Story* at $7.95* each. I'm sending you a check for $_____, made out to CharisMissions.

   *Note: If you live in California, add $0.54 sales tax per copy ordered. If your order comes from outside the U.S.A., add $2.00 for shipping for each copy ordered.

☐ I would like to bring the Spanish ministries of CharisMissions to my community; please send me information.

☐ Please, send me your catalog of Spanish cassettes, books, and videos.

☐ I would like to support the work of CharisMissions. Please send me information describing how I can help.

☐ Keep me posted on upcoming events of CharisMissions.

Name: _____

Address: _____

City _____

State: _____ Zip Code: _____

Telephone: _____

Send this order form to:

CharisMissions
P.O Box 947
Montebello, CA 90640

Special Introductory Offer

NEW COVENANT

The Magazine of Catholic Renewal

Month by month, *New Covenant* will bring you inspiration, teaching, and personal testimony that will help you:

- deepen your prayer life
- better understand your Catholic faith
- live as a Christian in today's world

Just write to the address below for a free copy of *New Covenant*. If you like what you see, pay the invoice and you'll receive eleven more copies–one year of *New Covenant* for only $14.95.

NEW COVENANT
Department S
P.O. Box 7009
Ann Arbor, MI 48107

Books of Interest by Mother Teresa

Total Surrender
Total Surrender probes beyond the popular image of Mother Teresa to the very heart of her spiritual life and mission. In her own words, Mother Teresa tells of the simple joy of following Jesus and surrendering fully to him. *$4.95*

Heart of Joy
These are the writings and teachings of a woman whose works and words have touched more people than any other woman living today. *$4.95*

One Heart Full of Love
More stirring addresses and interviews given by Mother Teresa to her Missionaries of Charity and other groups worldwide on such topics as self-giving, the call to love our neighbor, and spiritual poverty in the West. *$4.95*

Available at your Christian bookstore or from:
**Servant Publications • Dept. 209 • P.O. Box 7455
Ann Arbor, Michigan 48107**
Please include payment plus $1.25 per book
for postage and handling.
*Send for our FREE catalog of Christian
books, music, and cassettes.*